DIY COLOUR SERIES

Outdoor
DIY PROJECTS

AURA
EDITIONS

CONTENTS

Editor: Mary Lambert
Art editor: Gordon Robertson

Published by Aura Editions
2 Derby Road, Greenford, Middlesex

Produced by Marshall Cavendish Books Limited
58 Old Compton Street, London W1V 5PA

© Marshall Cavendish Limited 1985

ISBN 0 86307 279 8

Printed and bound in Hong Kong by Dai Nippon Printing Company

While every care has been taken to ensure that the information in *Outdoor DIY Projects* is accurate,
individual circumstances may vary greatly. So proceed with caution,
especially where electrical, plumbing or structural work is involved.

CHAPTER 1

DECORATING AND RENOVATING

Repainting the exterior of your house may give a bright new look to your property but the effect isn't solely decorative. Thorough preparation of surfaces, a meticulous work routine and regular re-inspection of trouble-spots is necessary for lasting results. The walls are one of the areas most prone to deterioration through age and the constant battering from the weather: if brickwork has been allowed to fall foul of these faults, act now to put right the damage.

PAINTING THE OUTSIDE

The skill and experience you require to make a good job of painting the outside of your house are fairly minimal. However, what you do need in good measure are patience, tenacity and, unless you live in a bungalow, a head for heights.

Outdoor maintenance is a time consuming and, at times, messy job. Painting (or repainting) is only half the story; much of the time and effort is spent on preparation. Do this properly and the job may not need doing again for five years; skimp on the preparation and you will be back up the ladder in eighteen months time.

It's because the time element is such a big factor compared to the cost of materials that you can save so much money by doing the job yourself. The main disadvantage is that it will eat into your leisure time—to do a three-bedroom house properly from top to toe will take at least four weekends.

For a house that is in poor condition

you've no alternative but to tackle the whole job at once to get the paintwork back in order. But once you've got a reasonable finish, or if the house is not too bad to start with, it makes sense to split the house into areas and to deal with these by rotation each year—start at one end and work your way round. This approach makes the chore an annual one, but it keeps the task more manageable. Tackling the job in this way also ensures that no part deteriorates too badly before it gets attention.

It is the combined effect of moisture and sunshine that causes paint failures so, before you start, have a good look around the outside of your house to check its condition. Pay particular attention to those sides

Below: Repainting the outside of your home will really brighten it up and, more importantly, really protect it against all the adverse weather conditions

which bear the brunt of the elements.

Weighing up the job

Divide the job into woodwork and masonry.
Woodwork: Start by carefully inspecting the lower corner joints of window and door frames. This is where paint usually deteriorates first and where wood starts to rot. Test for rot with an old knife: if the wood is soft and wet you'll have to sort it out before starting to repaint (see Preparation). While looking at your windows, check the condition of the putty holding the glass in the frames. If it is cracked or missing, replace it first

The only satisfactory way of closely inspecting woodwork at roof height—the bargeboards, soffits and fascias—is on a ladder. If you don't own a ladder yourself, borrow one from a friend—it's not worth

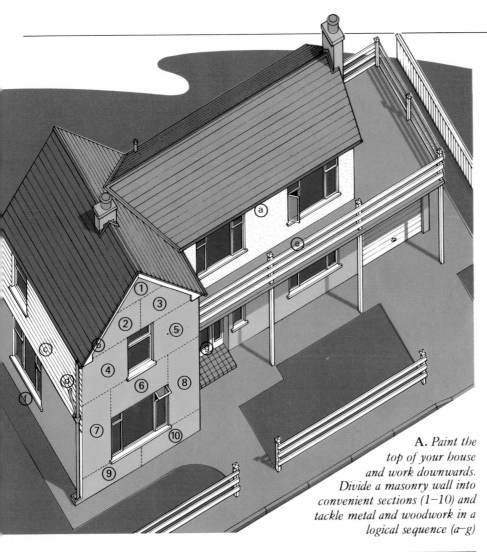

A. Paint the top of your house and work downwards. Divide a masonry wall into convenient sections (1–10) and tackle metal and woodwork in a logical sequence (a–g)

applied over a darker one.

You can also buy water-based gloss topcoat finish paints, which last at least as well as the best alkyd-resin based paints. The manufacturers claim that these paints allow the wood to breathe slightly by letting moisture through the paint film. Water-based topcoats tend not to be as glossy as alkyd-resin topcoats but they are well worth considering. Always buy primer and topcoat paint from the same manufacturer. Apart from giving better results, it may affect any guarantee.

On *masonry* the best choice is masonry paint, which contains crushed rock or synthetic fibre to reinforce the paint film and fill any small cracks. Another option is to use cement paint, which is sold as a powder for home mixing; however, it tends to be expensive and can't be used on a surface which has already been painted.

Tools and other materials

● You'll need access equipment for high-level work. An extension ladder—about 7m long for a two-storey house—will do, but you need a good head for heights to work at the top of a ladder. An access tower is safer and more comfortable if you have room to use one—you need a flat area next to the house at least 0.6m wide. Access towers are so much safer than ladders that it is worth making space where possible. You can hire access towers in easily assembled kit form.

When working aloft have an eye for safety—for the people below as well as yourself. Make sure that nothing can fall off the ladder or access tower. Never deliberately drop things to the ground. If necessary, cordon off the whole area.

● To prepare wood and metal surfaces, a stripping knife, hot air stripper (or blowtorch), wet and dry abrasive paper and filler are essential. You may also want to use a paint stripping chemical for fiddly areas around windows, such as the glazing bars, putty, sugar soap and possibly something to treat rot with—proprietary kits are sold for the purpose.

● To prepare masonry surfaces for

hiring one at this stage as, if you're lucky, the woodwork may not need repainting. As a last resort, you could try using binoculars to get a better view from ground level.

Metalwork: Rust is the main cause of peeling paint, so check downpipes and guttering (on a ladder) for blisters and cracks.

Masonry: A possible reason for badly flaking paint is damp. Don't attempt to cover such flaking, call in professional help to find the root cause. Mildly peeling paint can be scraped off and the masonry sealed with a stabilizing solution.

Types of paint

For *wood* and *metalwork* always examine the surface to see if it needs priming. Generally speaking, you will get the best performance by using separate special purpose primers for woodwork and for metal but if you use a universal primer you can do both wood and metal surfaces from one tin. A third choice are the quick-drying acrylic primers. These water-based paints cope with all surfaces and most can be

★ WATCH POINT ★

While examining your gutters, clear out any debris that may have collected in them over the years —blocked gutters are a main reason for damp walls.

overpainted in just three hours.

Gloss paint is traditionally used for the topcoats. There are two types of gloss paint —non-drip and liquid. Non-drip paints are applied in two coats over a primer; liquid glosses are conventionally applied as one coat on top of an undercoat applied over a primer. However, there is a school of thought which believes that undercoats are not only unnecessary but actually cause the paint to fail more rapidly because they are not flexible enough to take up movement by the wood and tend to crack. For this reason some professionals use two topcoats over primer for most exterior wood and introduce an undercoat only when the paintwork will be under particularly close scrutiny or if a light-coloured paint is being

★ WATCH POINT ★

A butcher's hook enables you to hang your paint pot from a convenient rung of the ladder instead of holding it. They're available from DIY and decorating shops.

painting, all you need is a stiff brush and maybe stabilizing and fungicidal solutions to treat dusty, powdery surfaces and eradicate mould spores respectively.

● What you use to apply the paint with is largely a matter of personal preference. If you prefer to use a brush for trim surfaces, a 50mm brush is the largest you will need although for narrow surfaces a 38mm or 25mm brush would be better. For edges you can use a cutting-in brush (sometimes called a sash brush), which has the bristles cut at an angle.

Paint pads are the other main option for painting woodwork and metalwork. Their chief advantage is that they don't splash. Their major disadvantage—that they give a disappointing finish with gloss—is often not important out of doors. Paint pads often come with a tray for loading, but if you use a brush you will need a paint kettle or some other wide-mouthed, shallow, easy-to-carry container to decant the paint into.

● For masonry paint, a paint roller or spraying equipment (fitted with a special nozzle) is faster than a brush but a brush is better for covering uneven surfaces. There are special brushes for masonry paint but the crushed stone in the paint will ruin good tools so use cheaper ones you don't care about or are prepared to throw out.

● Protective clothing is a must. You need gloves to protect your hands when using chemicals such as strippers or sugar soap and goggles when using chemicals or abrasives in a power tool of any sort.

1 *When the paint starts to blister, you will need to scrape it off, doing one layer at a time*

2 *Brush a wood hardener over any rotten or decaying areas of woodwork before you apply the filler*

4 *The quickest and easiest way to remove any flaking rust is with a disc sander*

5 *For downpipes, wrap wet and dry paper around a sponge—it will accommodate the curve*

Planning the job

The best way to work is from the top down (fig. A)—that way debris and splashes won't fall on parts you have freshly painted. It also gets the worst over and done with first—and if you're going to hire a ladder or access tower, it means you can take back the equipment as soon as possible to cut down on hire costs.

Aim to paint when it has been dry for a few days and looks set to stay fair for a few more. Paint can be damaged by frost and by blistering sun so avoid days when either of these is forecast. On sunny days try to work in the shade. Above all, avoid windy days as the wind will pick up debris and deposit it on wet paint. If dirt particles do settle on the surface, you will have to let the paint dry before sanding them off and repainting.

If you are painting the walls as well as the trim—the woodwork and metalwork—think about a logical order which will suit you. Painting the walls is probably more

★ WATCH POINT ★

Old bedspreads make ideal dust-sheets. Jumble sales are a good source. Plastic sheeting is an alternative but needs to be firmly weighted down.

splashy so do them first and then the trim. Whatever the order, work carefully to avoid splashes and cover vulnerable areas with large dustsheets. Paving and flowerbeds in reach of splashing also need covering.

Preparation

Although it is tedious, thorough preparation is the key to successful results: before you start painting, carry out the necessary surface repairs.

Woodwork: Deal with peeling areas first by taking off all the loose and flaking paint.

The best way to do this is with an electric hot air stripper (fig. 1) or to burn it off with a blowtorch. Provided you have a long enough extension lead, the electric tool has several advantages; it can be used closer to glass, can cope with mouldings and won't scorch the wood. It is also safer than a naked flame.

Play the hot air or flame over the paint and, once it has melted, scrape it from the surface. If you do use a blowtorch, keep a plastic bottle of water handy in case of fire and take particular care at the eaves of the house where birds' nests may be hidden—they ignite in a flash and can set the whole roof alight. Around the glass of window frames you will have to resort to paint stripper, use abrasive paper wrapped around a block or use a dry-stripping tool.

If you discover any rotten wood, don't despair. The traditional way of dealing with rotten wood is to cut out the bad and replace it with a new section of preservative-treated wood. As most bits of wood are shaped mouldings, this usually means chiselling or

3 *Patch the damaged area with the repairing filler as smoothly as possible, then treat with preservative rods*

6 *Brush down masonry and, if it's still flaky and dusty, prime it with a stabilizing solution*

routing it to match the existing frame. However, for do-it-yourselfers who aren't skilled in carpentry, there are now two easier methods: one is to squirt a resin into the damaged wood and to let it harden, thus restoring strength to the wood; and the other is to use a rot treatment system: these typically include a hardener, a filler and preservative rods. To use a kit, first cut away the rotten wood before painting the hardener on to the surface (fig. 2) and filling the hollow (fig. 3). The preservative rods are inserted into the wood in drilled holes around the repair to protect it from further damage.

Fill any cracks or holes in sound wood with an exterior-grade wood filler. Where a good finish is important—such as on a ground-floor window sill—use the filler to raise the level (where the paint has been removed) back to the level of the sound paint. The difference is only a fraction, but if you are too hasty, it will always look patchy. If the joints of a frame or door have moved apart, force a flexible mastic-type filler into

the gaps. The resilience of this type of filler will allow it to take up any further movement in the wood.

If you come across cracked or damaged putty, don't be tempted to paint over it; it's much better to scrape it away and reputty (see Renewing putty).

Rub down the stripped wood and filled patches with a fine grade—120g—glass-paper. Wood that has been exposed for even a short while will have developed a weathered surface which must be sanded off.

Before painting over sound paintwork use an old paintbrush and a weak solution of sugar soap to clean off dirt. Other washing solutions such as detergent, soap powder or washing soda can be used, but sugar soap is easiest to rinse off completely—this is important because any residue will slow down or even prevent the paint from drying. Remember to clean (and later on, paint) the inside edges of opening windows. Rinse and then use wet and dry abrasive paper and water to rub down the surface. Rinse again to remove the grey flecks of abrasive and let the surface dry.

Metal frames: If paint is flaking off metal-work, the surface below will probably be rusty. This spells trouble and means a lot of work getting it back to a clean surface. There are special treatments for painting over rust which are claimed to inhibit its spread, but there is really no substitute for sanding it off.

For quick results use a silicon carbide disc fitted to a sanding attachment on a power drill. Where the disc will not reach or fit, try a small wire brush in a power drill and as a last resort for really fiddly or intricate areas use coarse wire wool by hand. Wash off all the debris and let the surface dry before priming with zinc phosphate primer.

Sound paintwork over metal can be cleaned with a sugar soap solution, as for woodwork, and repainted.

Apart from rust problems, there will be no need to remove paint from metalwork unless a build up of coats is causing an opening window to stick. If this is the case find out whether the window is plain steel or galvanized—if you've no problems with rust on any other metalwork (or when in doubt) assume that it is galvanized. It is best to leave galvanized steel alone as any stripping could damage the galvanizing coat and cause rust later on. For plain steel use a chemical paintstripper: wear gloves and goggles and stipple the stripper on to the paint with an old brush. Leave the stripper for the specified time—usually ten minutes —and then scrape it off carefully.

As with wood windows, look out for crumbly, loose putty on metal frames, too. Replace with new putty before repainting the frame (see Renewing putty).

Metal guttering and downpipes: If any metal guttering is in bad condition, consider replacing it with plastic, which never needs to be painted—it will be worthwhile in the long run. Otherwise treat rust as described above, by removing flaking areas with an abrasive disc attachment to an electric drill (fig. 4). For downpipes, wrap wet and dry abrasive paper round a sponge—it accommodates the curve (fig. 5).

Wash down sound paint with sugar soap solution. Check whether black paint is bituminous or not. If it is, and it's in good condition, leave it alone: bituminous paint forms a valuable protective layer. If you want to paint over bituminous paint, you must seal it first with aluminium primer or the original surface may bleed through your new finish.

Masonry: Use a stiff fibre or plastic brush (not a wire brush) to clean down the masonry and remove any loose bits. If the brush pulls a lot of material off, it shows that the surface is friable (decaying to powder) and will need priming with a stabilizing solution (fig. 6). Algae on masonry will stop the paint from adhering and will need to be washed with a fungicidal solution or diluted bleach.

If the wall is rendered or pebble-dashed make good any damage before proceeding. With brickwork check the pointing.

Renewing putty

Make sure that you buy the right putty for your window—they're not all the same. Metal frames require a different kind to the usual linseed oil-based wood putty, called metal casement putty.

Glaziers use a special hacking knife for removing defective putty but if you haven't got one, use an old chisel to prise off loose or cracked material (fig. 7). Remove only as much as you need and then clean out the rebate with a brush. Paint the inside of the rebate with primer and leave it to dry out thoroughly.

If you have a wooden window, take the opportunity while the putty is removed to have a good look at the sprigs—the small metal nails which hold the glass in place. If any are loose or rusty, knock in replacements with a pin hammer. Be very careful, as it's all too easy to smash the pane.

A professional glazier will roll a small handful of putty into a ball and, holding it in

7 *Remove cracked putty by levering it off with an old chisel or screwdriver*

8 *The easiest way to apply putty is to roll sausages and use them to line the rebate*

9 *Bevel the putty to form a seal against the glass. Let putty dry out before painting*

10 *Apply shellac knotting to seal 'live' knots which have never been painted*

11 *Prime bare wood and if you are renewing putty, paint the rebate*

12 *Sand down lightly after each coat with wet and dry paper on a block*

13 *Brush on the topcoat with even strokes to get a really smooth finish*

14 *Use a brush for painting uneven masonry. If necessary, apply two coats*

the palm of his hand, feed the putty through finger and thumb into the rebate. This is more difficult than it sounds and if you can't handle it try rolling out a sausage of putty first and use that to line the rebate (fig. 8).

Fresh putty is often wet with oil and tends to stick to your fingers instead of becoming pliable. Work in any oil which is noticeable on the top of a new tin and if it is still sticky, roll it out on a clean stone to remove any excess oil.

Level off the putty to form a bevel against the glass. A putty knife is normally used for this (fig. 9) but almost any flexible knife will do. Putty dries by contact with the air so don't paint over it for two weeks or so. When you do overpaint, carry the paint right over the edge of the putty by about 3mm to form a compact seal against the pane of glass.

Starting to paint

Before you start repainting, lay down your protective dustsheets on the ground below—they will save you a lot of time and bother clearing up any unwanted splashes of paint afterwards.

Wood: Apply shellac knotting to any knots which have never been painted (fig. 10) and then prime all bare wood (fig. 11). When you paint around glass hold a piece of card or a proprietary plastic or metal paint shield along the edge.

Most outdoor wooden surfaces are narrow so they are not too difficult to paint. For the best results spread the paint fairly thickly, taking particular care to cover the edges. Load the brush by dipping one-third of the bristle length into the paint and remove the excess by pressing both sides of the brush against the side of the container. Starting with the primer, put dabs of paint on the surface at 50mm to 60mm spaces. Then join the dabs together with several firm brush strokes, followed by light strokes parallel to the length of the frame. These last strokes should then just pull the top

★ WATCH POINT ★

When you paint downpipes, you will find it easier to hold a piece of card or newspaper behind them to protect the wall surface from any unsightly paint splashes.

surface right into line.

When the primer is dry—about 24 hours with an alkyd—use a fine-grade abrasive to rub down. Don't apply a lot of pressure and take care not to rub the paint thin (fig. 12). Follow the primer with the undercoat or first topcoat (fig. 13). Allow each coat to dry before rubbing it down lightly with a fine abrasive. Take most care with the application of the topcoat as it will be the layer on show, but remember not to skimp on the earlier stages.

Metalwork: Pipes and gutters are painted in much the same way as wood if you are using gloss paint. Bituminous paint goes on in two or three fairly thick coats with a large brush—it will ruin a new brush so use an old one.

Masonry: Brush, roll or spray on the paint, working on an area about two square metres at a time (fig. 14). One coat may be enough cover for some walls but it is often advisable to do two for a better, more professional finish.

For the bottom 300mm or so of the walls, you can use a bituminous paint to give a black plinth. Not only does this look effective but it also hides splashes which would otherwise disfigure a light coloured masonry paint.

REPOINTING BRICKWORK

The mortar joints in brickwork protect a wall from the damaging effects of rainwater. So if the mortar shows signs of decay, replace it with fresh mortar to make a new seal.

So long as brickwork is correctly designed and well built, it does not require much in the way of maintenance or repair work. But, as a building ages, the mortar joints between the bricks may begin to decay and crumble. Flaking joints in brickwork allow water to penetrate the wall and should never be neglected. The remedy for crumbling joints is repointing—clearing out the old mortar a short way and replacing it with fresh mortar to make a new waterproof seal.

Types of joint

The mortar between bricks can be finished in one of several ways; wherever possible, you should try to match new joints to the existing ones. However, if the old mortar is particularly badly decayed, you may not be able to see what type of joint has been used.

Weather-struck joint (A): The horizontal joints of this type have sloped surfaces which are slightly recessed below the upper brick and slightly overhanging the lower one. This slope allows water to run off quickly and prevents it from lodging on the lower edge of the joints, thus giving the wall further protection from rain and moisture. The vertical joints slope from one side to the other and match the angle of the horizontals above and below. Other types of joint commonly used in brickwork include:

Flush joint (B): When the mortar has almost dried, it is rubbed over with a piece of wood or old sacking to produce a surface flush with the surrounding brickwork. This type of pointing looks particularly effective when used in conjunction with smooth-surfaced bricks.

Keyed or rounded joint (C): This is produced by running along the surface of the mortar with a semi-circular piece of metal to form a shallow, curved depression.

Recessed joint (D): This is formed by scraping out the freshly laid mortar to a depth of about 6mm below the brick surface, then smoothing the surface of the

Right: *This mortar is in bad need of repair—if left for very much longer rainwater will seep through and damp problems will occur*

remaining mortar with a piece of wood the width of the joint. Recessed joints look best on rough-textured bricks but should be used only where they match the existing pointing. If used on external walls in cold climates, the bricks must be hard and durable, otherwise water may collect and freeze on the ledges causing pieces of brick to flake off.

Equipment

For repointing brickwork, even if you are working over quite a small area of wall, you need a spot board on which to mix the

★ WATCH POINT ★

A suitable frenchman can be made from an old kitchen knife. Use a hacksaw to cut off the end of the knife, smooth off any burrs around the cut with a file, then heat the tip and bend it into a right-angle about 12mm from the end.

mortar and a hawk for carrying the mortar to the work area. For applying the mortar to the joints, you need a pointing trowel, which resembles a small bricklayer's trowel and for clearing out the old mortar, use an old shavehook with its pointed end cut off square or a special plugging chisel, made for the purpose.

If you are applying weather-struck joints, you also need a tool called a *frenchman* for trimming away the excess mortar at the bottom of the horizontal joints.

To guide the frenchman neatly along the joints when trimming, you need a straight-edged piece of timber which is held immediately below the top edge of the lower brick. Attach two pieces of hardboard to each end of the piece of wood so that when it is held against the wall, there is a slight gap allowing the trimmed mortar to fall through (fig. E).

Wherever possible, the mortar for repointing should be mixed to match the composition of the existing mortar. If you do not know the mixing proportions of the original mortar, use a 1:1:6 (cement:lime:sand) mix or 1 part of masonry cement to 3 parts of sand. An

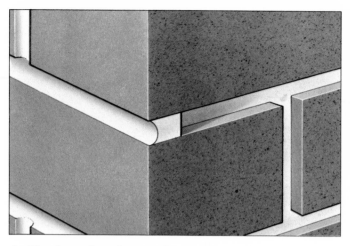

A. *The slope of weather-struck joints allows water to run off quickly, protecting the wall from rain*

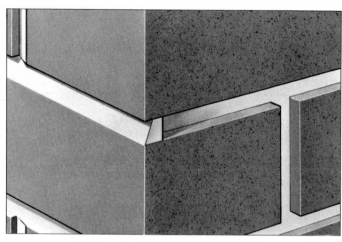

B. *Flush joints are produced by rubbing the mortar with a piece of wood to form a smooth surface*

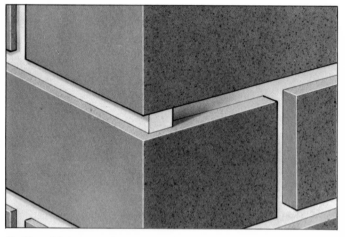

C. *Keyed joints are formed by smoothing the surface of the mortar with a rounded piece of metal*

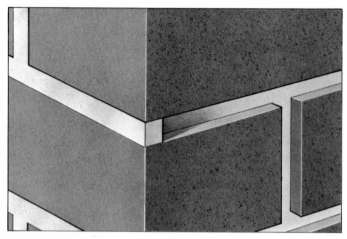

D. *The mortar in recessed joints is scraped out to a depth of about 6mm below the brick surface*

exception to the rule is the softer type of facing brick, where you should use a weaker 1:2:9 mix.

Use as fine a grade of sand as possible. If the only sand available is coarse, work it through a fine-meshed sieve to remove any pebbles.

Working considerations

Repointing is generally best undertaken during warm weather, as newly laid mortar is easily damaged by frost, particularly if you are using a weak mortar mix.

If the area to be pointed is large, tackle the work in stages, finishing off the joints over an area of about 2m² before moving on to the next. Start work at the top left hand corner of the wall and move across and downwards.

Mortar for pointing should be mixed in small batches and then used immediately. If you do mix too much, and some begins to

E. *To trim the excess mortar from the bottom of the weather-struck joints, use a frenchman and draw it along the top edge of a straight length of timber held just below the top edge of the lower brick. Attach a thin block of wood to each end of the timber to let the trimmed mortar fall through the gap. Make a frenchman from an old kitchen knife*

dry out and harden before you come to use it, discard it and mix a fresh batch. Do not try to reconstitute hardening mortar by adding more water to it.

Preparing the surface

If there is paving below the wall to be repointed, lay down a large sheet of polythene before you start work to protect the concrete path from mortar droppings.

With the protective sheeting in place, gently scrape any lichen and moss from the surface of the brickwork, taking care not to damage the faces of any bricks.

When the brickwork is clean, start raking the joints, using the cut-back shavehook or a plugging chisel, to a depth of between 12mm and 20mm—if you clear out the mortar further than this, you may damage the wall. Rake out the vertical joints—called *perpends*—first and then the horizontal, or *bed*, joints again taking care as you work not to damage the bricks.

Make sure that the recess formed in the joints is absolutely square and that no traces of old mortar remain on the edges of the bricks (fig. 1). If you fail to remove all the old mortar, the fresh mortar will not adhere properly and will soon flake and crumble.

When all the joints in the area to be repointed have been raked out, brush them thoroughly with a stiff hand brush to remove any remaining particles and dust (fig. 2).

In order to prevent too much moisture being absorbed by the surrounding brickwork from the fresh mortar, dampen the wall by flicking thoroughly clean water over the surface with a distemper brush (fig. 3). However, take care not to use too much water or you will soak the brickwork and the fresh mortar will not adhere properly.

Handling the trowel

Opinions vary on the best way of using a pointing trowel, so it is best to experiment until you find a style that suits you before you start.

You may find that the easiest method is to roll the mortar down the hawk and divide it into 'strands' as long as the trowel and about 12mm thick (fig. 5). Pick up each strand on the back of the trowel, along one edge, and flick it firmly into the waiting joint (fig. 6).

Weather-struck joints

Although slightly more difficult to construct than other types of brick joint, weather-struck joints are well worth the extra trouble as they give the wall added protection against water penetration.

To fashion weather-struck joints, start by transferring a manageable amount of mortar from the spot board to the hawk and carry it to the work area. Using the pointing trowel, force some mortar well into the first few perpends. Use the trowel to form a sloping angle by drawing it down the edge of the brick on the right-hand side of the joint, then cut off the excess mortar neatly with the edge of the trowel (fig. 7).

Move on to the bed joints above and below the filled perpends. Holding the trowel point upwards, press in more mortar, so that it is recessed to a depth of about 3mm at the top of the gap and slightly overhangs the edge of the brick at the bottom (fig. 8).

When you have used up the first batch

1 *To prepare the surface of brickwork for repointing, rake out some of the old mortar from the joints with an old shavehook*

2 *Make sure that no traces of old mortar are left at the edges and brush down the joints to remove any remaining dust*

3 *Dampen the surface of the brickwork with a distemper brush and clean water to make sure that the new mortar will bond*

4 *Mix up your first batch of mortar taking care not to prepare too much. Try to match the composition of the mix with that of the old mortar*

of mortar, make the rough slope already formed in the perpends neater by trimming off any remaining excess with the pointing trowel so the mortar is recessed 3mm on the right-hand side.

Next, take the frenchman and straightedge to the wall. Holding the straightedge immediately below the lower edge of the bed joints, run the frenchman along the wall, with its tip pointing downwards, to cut off the excess mortar (fig. 9).

When the mortar has begun to harden, rub the joints with a dusting brush to remove any remaining waste then move on to the next section.

Flush and keyed joints

Pointing brickwork with flush joints pro-

vides a neat finish and can be particularly useful on old brickwork, where the outer corners of the bricks have crumbled and the wall surface is to be redecorated.

Start as for weather-struck joints by filling perpends then bed joints. Press the mortar firmly into place with the pointing trowel, until it protrudes slightly out from the surface of the brickwork.

When the mortar starts to harden, rub along the joints with a piece of wood or old sacking working in the same direction, until the mortar is flush with the surrounding brickwork. When completely dry, scrape over the mortar with a stiff piece of plastic to remove any excess particles of mortar dust.

To form a keyed joint, press the mortar well into the joints with the trowel, then smooth it to shape with a piece of metal rod, wooden dowelling or a piece of unridged

5 *Transfer a manageable amount of mortar to the hawk and divide it into strands as long as the trowel and about 12mm thick*

6 *Carry the hawk to the work area and pick up strands of mortar with the back of the pointing trowel. Force the mortar into the joints*

7 *If you are making weather-struck joints, form the sloping angle in the perpends by drawing the trowel down the edge of the brick*

8 *Tuck the mortar into the beds of weather-struck joints so that it is recessed under the top brick and slightly overhangs the lower one*

9 *Trim off the excess mortar at the bottom of the weather-struck joints with a frenchman, then brush the joints to remove waste*

10 *If you are making recessed joints use a shavehook, with its point cut off, to scrape out the freshly laid mortar*

garden hose. After rubbing the joints, trim the surplus mortar with the trowel.

Cleaning the brickwork

Although all the joints should be cleaned off as thoroughly as possible during the pointing process, it is difficult to achieve a completely clean finish by this means alone and some mortar will probably be left adhering to the edges of the bricks.

If marks still remain on the brickwork because the mortar has penetrated the surface, they can be removed with a very dilute solution of hydrochloric acid—1:10 by volume for clay bricks and 1:2 by volume for calcium silicate bricks. Saturate the brickwork with clean water, then apply the solution sparingly with an old paint-brush, taking great care not to get any on

★ WATCH POINT ★

Never try to remove mortar which has been spattered on bricks while it is still wet, or attempt to wash it off with water. Instead, leave the excess mortar to dry out completely then use a stiff scrubbing brush to brush the soiled bricks. Remove large lumps of mortar on clay bricks by scraping with the side of a trowel. With calcium silicate bricks, lightly abrade the surface with a brick of the same colour to remove large pieces.

your skin or in your eyes. When the area has been thoroughly treated, hose down the brickwork to remove every trace. The surface of some types of brick can be affected

by acid so, if in doubt, seek expert advice.

Colouring joints

To produce a matching or decorative effect in finished brickwork, proprietary colour-ants and special coloured cements are all available from builders' merchants and can be added to the mortar mix if desired. But because the colour will be altered by the texture of ordinary sand, you should use white sand in the mix, if possible. Remember also that cement with colour additives requires less water.

If you are repointing part of a wall and want the colour of the fresh mortar to match that in the existing joints, rub the joints around the area with candlewax to prevent them from absorbing the colouring in the new mortar mixture.

CHAPTER 2

SHUTTERS AND BLINDS

Most of us welcome the summer sunshine. But it is also nice to escape indoors from the heat and glare. Window shutters not only add style to the outside appearance of the house but also keep exposed rooms cool in the heat of the day, protecting furnishings from the fading effects of the sun's rays. A sunblind or awning does likewise, plus casting welcome shade for outdoor meals on the patio.

FIT ORNAMENTAL SHUTTERS

Shutters can be used to brighten a plain house front or add charm to a country cottage. You can make and fit them as decorative panels or as working, hinged, flaps to keep the sun's glare from south-facing rooms.

You can buy shutters ready-made, but there is not a great deal of choice. So making them yourself makes sense—especially as DIY shutters are much cheaper than store-bought ones. You can design them to suit the individual style of your house and to fit your window sizes exactly.

When it comes to matching home-made shutters to the style of your house you also get a choice of finishes. You can stain the shutters, leave them natural or paint them to match your window and door frames.

Choosing a style

It is important to choose a style of shutter which matches the style of your house. Modern ranch-style houses call for louvred shutters, ultra-modern houses will need slim-line frames and suburban Tudor homes call for much heavier framing. Mock

Below: *Shutters come in many different styles and can either be purely decorative or they can shield the glare of the sun*

Gothic and those homes built in a rural brick and tile style particularly suit the popular, and easy-to-make, tongued-and-grooved, plain or V-jointed boarding.

The wood required to make your own shutters in this style is readily available in widths of 100mm to 150mm and thicknesses of between 16mm and 20mm. Panelling in these sizes is not too heavy to handle and, if you provide some bracing behind it, sufficiently sturdy for the job.

If you prefer a boarding with a profile, try to use boards of roughly the same dimensions. Do not use man-made boarding for this job—only expensive marine ply is suitable for outside use and even then its

edges need to be sealed. Whichever material you do use, however, make sure that all the surfaces are treated thoroughly with wood preservative.

Choosing the fittings

The right fittings will make all the difference to the finish of your shutters. Although the fittings for fixed shutters serve no practical purpose, to achieve the effect you want the fittings need to look as sturdy as those used for the real things. Working shutters will obviously need sturdy fittings—particularly the hinges. Have a look around your local builders' merchant for old-style fittings—some manufacturers still haven't changed the original designs. Err on the side of heaviness and over-size.

If you feel that the finished shutters will look too plain, consider making some simple decorative cut-outs in them. These can be made by hand but using a powered jig saw makes the job a lot easier. Fig. C shows three typical styles of shutter decoration.

Planning

From the outside of your house, look at the area around the windows to make sure that fitting shutters is feasible. Downpipes, climbing roses and nearby trees may all hinder your plans.

If you have outward opening casement windows, you will only be able to open and close the shutters by going outside—an obvious drawback with windows situated on the first floor.

Imagine how your house will look once the shutters are fitted. Never fit shutters to one window only unless you have a house where that window can be viewed only in isolation.

Plan to make your shutters the same depth as the window opening—even if they're fixed, they should look as though they would cover the depth if needed. But it's not necessary to make fixed shutters exactly half the width of the opening—any discrepancy here is less noticeable and helps you by cutting down on the wood and all the work involved.

A. *Shutters can be all things to all houses, but it's important visually to match the shutters to the house. Half-timbered houses don't suit louvred shutters, and modern houses don't suit old oak*

Treating the timber

Timber that's going to be used outdoors must be treated thoroughly to protect it for all kinds of weather. Your aim is to get the timber to absorb as much preservative as possible, so make sure the timber is dry. The best time to treat it is after you have cut

★ WATCH POINT ★

One way to ensure that end grain is well soaked is to stand the pieces in a big tin or small bucket of preservative and brush the liquid up them frequently. Leave them for about two days—one each end (fig. 1).

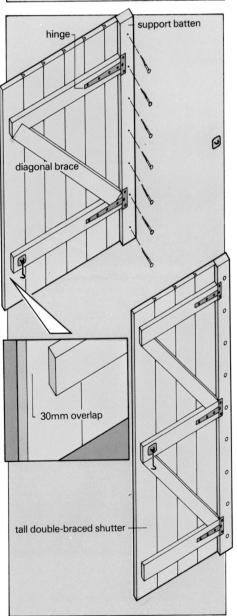

hinge

support batten

diagonal brace

30mm overlap

tall double-braced shutter

the timber to size and made any cut-outs or cut any joints.

Manufacturers' instructions will vary but ordinary preservative should be applied with a big, full brush. But it's not like painting: aim to flood the surface, including any cuts and endgrain.

You can apply preservative yourself or buy timber ready-impregnated—it will cost a little more but reputable builders use it as a matter of course. It's a little more difficult to find for the home builder.

The treatment you choose will depend on how you want your shutters to look. Creosote is the traditional finish and these days you can get it in a range of brownish shades—from light to dark. Remember that you won't be able to paint over it later.

Water-repellent preservatives come in clear, or in a range of colours (fig. 2). They usually have a fungus and insect repellent in them as well. The coloured versions are good if you want the grain to show.

There are also clear, tinted preservatives which can alter the character of timber drastically, making pine look like oak, for example.

Exterior varnishes have been traditional in boat building and there's no reason why you shouldn't use them on your shutters. Opt for matt varnishes, however: glossy shutters will look odd.

Painting is an equally traditional finish for shutters (fig. 3). You'll have to use preservatives under the paint coats, so check when you are buying them that they will allow painting on top.

A word on aesthetic considerations: shutters can look good whatever style you choose, but the wrong choice of colours can be a serious design mistake. Shutters should, if possible, complement doors, window frames and exterior woodwork, so you may find that a totally different colour scheme is required.

Remember that bright primary colours look good in small areas like the door or window frames, while large shutters painted to match may simply look garish. Think about this very carefully and try to make a colour sketch of how the house will look. If you do feel that it is necessary to repaint the door and window frames, don't be put off: the finished overall effect, once the shutters are erected, should be more than the sum of its parts.

B. *Working shutters need substantial reinforcement to prevent sagging. An angled brace will do the job (top). Tall shutters need double bracing to stop tongued and grooved boarding from pulling apart*

Measuring up

Measure the dimensions of your window openings before you buy any materials. It's the size of the opening in the brickwork or timber that you are concerned with—not the size of the window itself.

Measure the height and width of each opening. Shutters should be made 15mm longer than the height so that if they were shut they would just conceal the top of the reveal. Make working shutters half the width of the opening, less about 5mm for clearance; fixed shutters less than half.

When you are working out the number of boards required, remember that you have to saw off the tongue on one side of each shutter and the groove on the other.

The chances are, with working shutters, that you will end up needing a half or quarter width board in each shutter. You may be able to get around this by using

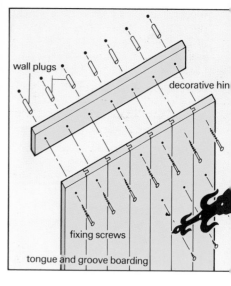

> C. Decorative styles of shutters:
> A. Cut out design in timber. B. Chunky hinges. C. Iron studs

> D. Fake shutters can be screwed to the wall through the backing piece while decorative hinges are screwed to the front

boards of a different width—sizes vary between 100mm and 150mm—or by adjusting the position of the hinges in relation to the opening. But if you can't solve the problem this way you will have to cut a board lengthwise using a ripsaw, then plane off the edge neatly. The cut board should go on the hinge side of the shutter.

Estimate the length of tongued, grooved and V-jointed boarding you will need for each shutter by multiplying its height by the number of boards to make the span. You will also need four 75mm × 25mm softwood boards for the horizontal rails—the width of each shutter less 30mm. Working shutters also need two 75mm × 25mm pieces for the diagonal braces. As a rough guide for their length, simply measure the diagonal of a shutter and multiply by two.

Finally, you will need two 50mm × 50mm pieces the height of the shutter for the side battens to which you fix the hinges.

Assembling the shutters

The shutters are simply panels of tongued-and-grooved and V-jointed boarding held

1 Stand the boards in a bucket of preservative to flood the end grain, and apply to the rest using an old brush

2 If creosote is too sombre for you there are other tinted clear preservatives you can use instead

5 Mark off and cut the boards using a tenon saw. Cut on the excess side of line and don't splinter protruding pieces

6 Saw or plane the tongues and grooves off the edges of the outside boards before screwing the backing piece down

together at the back with horizontal rails (fig. D). Working shutters also require diagonal braces (fig. B).

Start by cutting the boards all to the same length to suit your opening. Knock the boards together and level them at one end. Square them off at the other end (fig. 4) then saw off the excess (fig. 5). Saw and plane off the tongues of two of the boards and the grooves of two others. These will be the edge boards for the two shutters. Working on a flat surface, one shutter at a time, tap the tongues into the adjacent grooves of the boards to form a single leaf.

Measure and cut the horizontal rails. They should finish flush with the hinge side of the boards about 30mm in from the other side; for working shutters you will need to cut diagonal braces as well, plus two side battens to hinge them to the wall. For medium-sized shutters you can simply butt the slanting ends of the braces against the inner edges of the horizontal rails.

Remember that the diagonals should have their foot near the hinge—then the top effectively props up the outer end of the top rail.

If your shutters are tall and thin you will need to add a third horizontal rail in the middle and use two diagonal braces. And if they are big and heavy, it is sensible to cut a

---

★ WATCH POINT ★

To ensure that the rails and any braces are in the right position, temporarily tack the ends of the rails to the end boards and carefully turn over the whole shutter—the tongues and grooves should keep it all in one piece.

Nail the boards to the rails. As you nail keep a close check to see that the shutter remains square.

25mm deep triangle in the rails to provide a toehold for the diagonal braces. You will also need to trim off their points so they will fit. Alternatively, mitre the end of the diagonal.

With all the timber cut, it is time to treat the wood, as previously described. Make sure you treat each piece individually and don't miss any parts—especially end grain. After treatment let it dry and then start assembling the shutters.

Working on a flat surface assemble the treated boarding, tapping the tongues into the adjacent grooves. With one leaf assembled, mark the position of the horizontal rails and any diagonals and glue and screw or nail them into position from the other side (fig. 6).

Finishing off

Check that the tops and bottoms of the shutters are even and parallel. If there are any irregularities, mark a straight line as close as possible to the edge and use a circular saw or plane to get the top and bottom straight. Don't forget to give another coat of preservative to the end grain.

With the shutters made, it is time to add any decorative details in the form of handles or reproduction hinges or make cutouts or add decorative studs (figs 7 and 8).

You may find certain types of decorative studs and hinges can be fitted after the shutters are erected. If so, this is a bonus: it allows you to arrange the decoration when the shutter is in its proper place, and so choose the pattern which best complements the overall decorative and colour scheme. Remember to match patterns with existing features of the windows such as handles.

Touch up any poorly covered sections with timber preservative, then apply your final coat and any paint. You are now ready to screw fixed shutters directly to the house and to begin hanging working shutters.

Fitting the shutters

Fixed shutters can simply be screwed to the house wall. Remember these shutters are going to be out in all weathers, all year round. So you will need at least three screws per rail—more if the shutter is bigger than average.

Drill and countersink the shutters from the face side through the horizontal rails. Get a helper to hold a shutter in place while you mark through the screw holes directly on to the house wall.

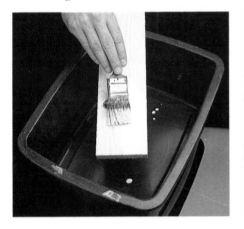

3 *If you wish to paint the shutters first apply a coat of primer, then undercoat and several topcoats*

4 *Knock the boards together with one end squared off. Mark any unevenness at the other end and remove the excess*

7 *Mark positions of decorations so that you can fix mounting screws where they are hidden when the shutter is fitted*

8 *Countersink the screw holes so that the heads will sit flush with the surface. You can conceal them with fittings*

Screw the shutters to the wall, using zinc-plated screws and wall plugs. Stand back and check that the shutters are positioned evenly on each side of the window opening and that they are level. Even if the opening is not quite square it is important that the top and bottom of the shutters are lined up with the most prominent horizontal feature (fig. 9)—the window sill or the eaves if they are just over the window opening—or a row of brickwork over the lintel. Then fit any decorative studs you are using in the screw holes (fig. 10).

With working shutters, it's easier if you do all the preliminaries on the ground. Lay the two shutters in their closed position on a flat surface and separate them with some 10mm to 15mm wide timber scraps to keep the gap parallel. Lay the two side battens on either side and line them with the top (fig. 11). The next task is to lay the hinges in the right position.

Nail a length of 50mm × 25mm timber temporarily across the top and bottom of the shutters and side battens to make the assembly rigid. Fix the hinges with four screws each (fig. 12).

Measure the width of shutters and battens and transfer this dimension to the window opening, making sure that the overlaps on either side are equal. Drill the side battens for the fixing screws and hinges (fig. 13). With a helper, carefully lift up the shutters, side battens and the temporary pieces nailed on top and bottom to hold the assembly over the window. Support it with packing pieces resting on the window ledge, check for level and mark the screw holes through to the wall.

If the wall is brick use a masonry drill and tap in plastic wall plugs. Offer up the assembly and screw the side battens on to the wall before removing the temporary top and bottom ones.

Finishing touches

Because you have added painting and decorative features before you attached the shutters to the wall, the main finishing off work is touching up surfaces, filling and covering screw heads with decorative studs and fixing catches to working shutters.

The main functioning fittings left to add are those which hold the shutters open and hold them closed (fig. 14). The simplest method is to use two sets of cabin hooks and eyes. Close the shutters, hold the catch up to them and mark the position of the two parts and screw the catch into place.

Open the shutters and, using a second identical set, mark the positions on the wall: hook for the shutter cup on one side and cup for the shutter on the other.

If you add a security hasp, make sure it is attached to the inside of the shutters.

9 *Align the shutters with the most prominent feature—the window sill or the eaves—when screwing them to the wall*

10 *It is often helpful and easier to wait until the shutters are erected before fitting the fake hinges and studs*

11 *Lay working shutters side by side with an offcut setting the gap between them. Lay the side battens as well*

12 *Nail battens in place to hold the shutter assembly together temporarily. Then fit the hinges*

13 *Drill and countersink the fixing holes in the side battens before offering up the assembly for fixing*

14 *Working shutters will need catches and hooks so that they can be locked in an open or a closed position*

EXTERIOR SUNBLIND

A sunblind or awning is excellent for keeping south-facing rooms cool in summer. It can also be expensive to buy. As awnings must be made to measure anyway, save your money and make a pretty and practical one like this.

Simple awning

Picture windows, patio doors or French windows lighten your home and help open up the view to your garden, patio or courtyard. But if they face the rising or setting sun—or, in the northern hemisphere, they face south—then these windows can let in unwanted glare and heat during the summer months. Apart from the discomfort you might feel, that direct sunlight can also fade soft furnishings, or discolour varnished timber and even some paint surfaces.

One solution—popular throughout most south European countries—is to buy or build an awning. With a wealth of durable materials readily available, and in a variety of patterns and colours, a well-tailored awning can add that summery feeling to your property, neatly finish off the exterior of a window space and provide all the benefits of easily adjusted shade.

Proprietary awnings must be tailor made

Below: *A sunblind can be an inexpensive, attractive addition to patio doors or French windows*

to suit your window or patio door and, while a high standard of finish, materials and design is available, they'll inevitably cost you much more than making one yourself. And the beauty of building an awning is that it is a job every DIY enthusiast can handle without much difficulty.

Planning

Fig. A shows how the awning is constructed and how it is fitted to the wall. Because it is made to measure, you need to work out the dimensions to suit your window.

Choose your awning material carefully. You can safely use such materials as sail-

cloth or canvas (which you will need to treat), woven or proofed nylon. Select a reasonably heavyweight fabric so that it will not 'ripple' in strong breezes and run the risk of tearing when it is tacked to the awning frames. In some cases specific requirements for both design and colour will determine which fabric you end up using.

The easiest material to make the frames with—and the cheapest—is planed softwood batten. You will need to treat the timber with a preservative which can be painted or varnished over.

The mechanism for raising and lowering the awning is very straightforward. You will need a double and a single pulley block on a swivel mounting. These can be bought inexpensively from a chandlery or dinghy shop.

Your next step is to assess how the awning is to be fitted. If the exterior of your house—and in particular the area outside the window or patio door—is roughcast or pebble-dashed, you must provide a smooth surface against which the support frame for the awning can be secured. This means chipping away the finishing until you reach smooth brick or cement; you need to make good with repair mortar. Alternatively, pack out the frame and fill in behind.

Tools and materials

The frames are made entirely from PAR softwood in standard sizes. Actual dimensions will depend on the door or window you are building the frame around. You will need:
- 175mm × 25mm softwood for the wall box.
- 75mm × 25mm softwood for the wall frame.
- 50mm × 25mm softwood for the four moving frames.
- Enough awning material to cover the frames when fully opened, and go down the sides as well. The length of the material is the width of the frame plus twice the length of the frame sides. Its width (around the curve of the awning) is roughly 1.6 times the length of the frame sides. Add a little extra to allow for mistakes. If you can't get one piece large enough, you'll need to get two sewn together.
- Enough 6mm–10mm nylon rope to operate the pulley mechanism.
- 6 steel or backflap strap hinges to hold the frames together.
- 8 angle braces to strengthen frame joints.
- Enough 50mm No. 10 brass counter-

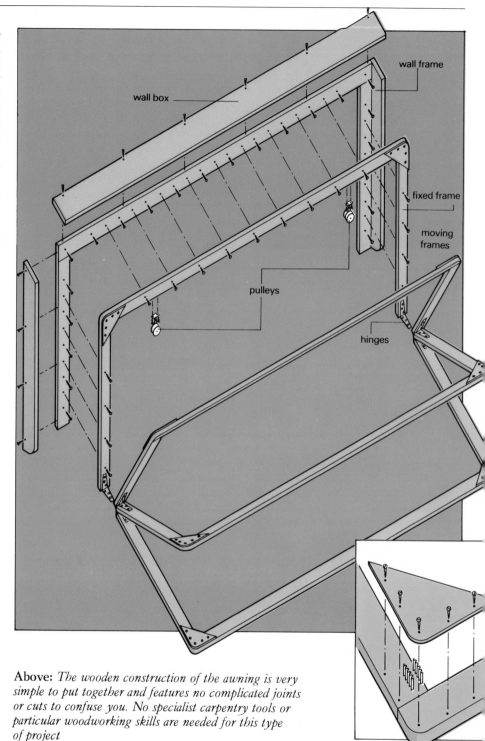

Above: *The wooden construction of the awning is very simple to put together and features no complicated joints or cuts to confuse you. No specialist carpentry tools or particular woodworking skills are needed for this type of project*

sunk woodscrews to hold the wall frame securely in place—you need one every 150mm—with plastic wall plugs to suit.
- Corrugated metal fasteners for frame connections.
- Single or double pulleys to make the pulley mechanism, rope to raise the frames and a cleat to tie off to.
- Woodscrews (38mm No. 8) and PVA woodworking adhesive for frame joints.
- Tacks and decorative upholstery pins to secure the awning material to the frames.

You will also need a tenon saw, a coping saw or power jig saw, screwdriver, drill and bits, a try square, a tack hammer, a 25mm bevel-edged chisel and medium-grade glasspaper for finishing. You must also use a waterproof adhesive such as urea formaldehyde to secure the joints.

Constructing the frames

Begin construction with the wall frame and

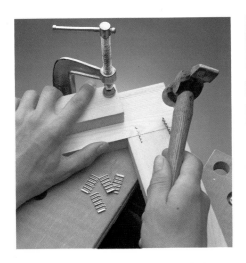

1 *Square up the frame joints and clamp them in place before securing them first with two corrugated metal fasteners*

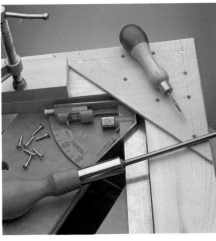

2 *Pre-drill the corner gussets, and glue and screw them in place. Use a square to ensure the corners are at right angles*

3 *Round off the corners—about 25mm is enough—to prevent the material tearing, then paint all the frames*

4 *Offer up the wall frame, mark its position, drill and plug the holes, then screw in place. Seal behind it with mastic*

remember that the dimensions of the top rail must allow for the length of the moving frames, plus 20mm clearance at each end. Measure the sections to be cut for the butt joints on both the top rail and side rails. The timber can be cut using a tenon saw, but make sure that the cut ends are exactly square.

Before joining the frame sections together, drill and countersink the screwholes for fitting the frame to the wall. You use 50mm No. 10 screws for this—either stainless steel or brass—so the clearance holes need to be 5mm diameter. Drill one hole every 150mm along the frame.

Arrange the top and side rails so that they are exactly square to each other, then fix them together using corrugated metal fasteners (fig. 1). Ensure, as you do so, that

they remain square. No further support is necessary as this frame will be fixed permanently to the wall.

From 175mm × 25mm planed softwood, cut out the wall box components which will be secured to the sides and top of the wall frame. Where the top and side edges meet, a simple butt joint will be adequate. Here the joints can be glued and screwed together.

★ WATCH POINT ★

If you wish, butt joints can be used and the corners secured with ply gussets (fig. 2) or, to gain additional strength, screw and glue offcut blocks into each corner.

Drill all the necessary screwholes and countersink them but do not, at this stage, fit to the wall frame.

Now follow the same procedure to construct four moving frames, checking that, when glued and screwed together, the frame sections remain at right-angles to one another.

Round off the top edges of the moving frames by sanding or with a planer file. In one of the frames, drill and countersink 45mm holes every 150mm. This will be the top-most frame and the holes will be used to fix it to the wall frame.

When all the frame components are completed, they should be treated with a suitable wood preservative then painted or varnished. Use a general purpose wood primer before painting, then apply undercoat and topcoat (fig. 3).

Before offering up and fitting the awning frames, check that all the joints are secure.

★ WATCH POINT ★

The pulley system will be connected up only when the awning material is in place. But when the frame is complete it is a good idea to fit the pulley blocks and securing cleat. The blocks should be screwed to the fixed frame about two thirds of the width of the awning apart. In the lowest moving frame, drill holes the same distance apart to allow the pulley rope to pass through and be knotted.

Offer up the wall frame, making sure it is square to the window opening, and mark the positions of the screw holes. Using a masonry bit (No. 10) drill the screw holes in the wall to at least 50mm deep. Offer up the wall frame and check that all the screw holes align.

Once the glue has dried fix the assembly to the wall using heavy-duty plastic wall plugs and for added water protection bed the frame on a sealant mastic (fig. 4). Do not attempt to secure the moving frames until you are sure that the wall frame is firmly fixed to the wall. Each of the moving frames must now be connected together using back-flap or strap hinges.

This is most easily done on a workbench or by laying the frames flat on the floor, fitting two hinges to the fixed frame, then screwing these hinges to the first moving frame (fig. 5). Stagger the hinges slightly so that the screws coming through one side of a frame member do not foul the screws coming through from the opposite side (fig. 6). Ensure the frames remain square and the hinges do not twist them out of shape.

Offer up the completed assembly (you will certainly need an assistant), and fix it temporarily to the wall frame.

Fitting the material

Before attempting to tack material to the awning, it must first be cut—and if wide enough sheets of the material cannot be obtained, lengths must be sewn together.

Open out the moving frames until the lowest frame is roughly horizontal. Now open out all the other frames equal distances apart (you will probably need some help for this) and tack two thin wooden battens across the inside of the ends of the frames, nailing to each one (fig. 7).

The material must first be secured behind the last, fixed frame. Take the frame off the wall frame in order to do this. Allow all the material to hang from the back of the frame, making sure that what will be the outside surface of the fabric is against the back of the frame where it is to be tacked (fig. 8).

B. *Stretch the material over the frame. Thinner fabrics need webbing tape to support the frames. Cut triangular gussets in situ. Fit up the pulley rope as shown*

Lay a strip of webbing over the tape so that it passes over the top edge of the frame and resecure the material by tacking again through the tape or webbing. Tack or staple the awning material to each of the frames in turn making sure the material is pulled taut, but not too tightly (fig. 9). The material must now be cut to match the side triangles.

Tack the material in place one frame at a time, stretching it slightly to prevent creases and cutting off the surplus as you go. Fig. B shows how the material is fitted and how the pulleys are fixed. Do not worry about the edges—they will be covered later. At the bottom of the lowest frame turn the material under the frame and tack it to the back edge. But leave the material slack each side of the holes drilled to take the pulley.

Now the moving frame assembly can be screwed to the wall frame by the holes in the topmost frame, using 38mm No. 8 screws.

With the awning in place you can now glue and screw the wall box top and side covers into position (fig. 11). Make sure that the awning with its material in place does not snag inside the wall box. If the fit is too tight, remove the folding frame assembly and reposition it as necessary until the fit is right.

A word of warning: many canvas-type materials will fray easily when you cut them. This isn't a problem where the frayed edge is tucked away out of sight, but

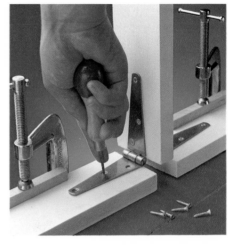

5 *Clamp frame members to a workbench and support intermediate ones while you fix the hinges in place*

8 *Run string lines between the frame corners while you stretch the material over the frames and pin it. Avoid wrinkles*

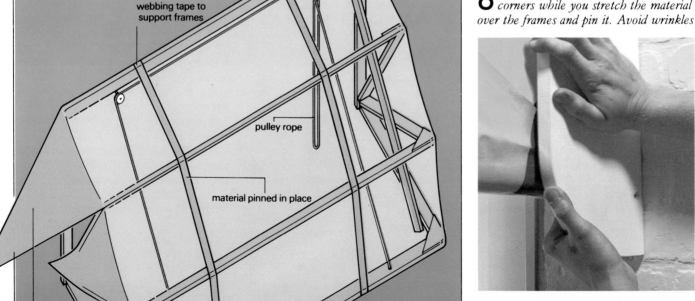

double pulley

temporary brace

webbing tape to support frames

pulley rope

material pinned in place

gussets cut in material

11 *Offer up the wall box components, then glue and screw them to the wall frame using mastic to seal the gap*

6 *Stagger the hinge positions slightly so that fixing screws on opposite sides of a frame member do not foul each other*

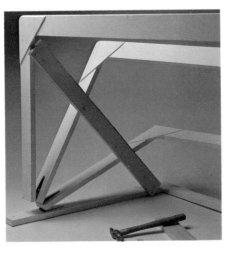

7 *Open out the four awning frames and hold them at the correct spacing with a wooden brace while fitting the material*

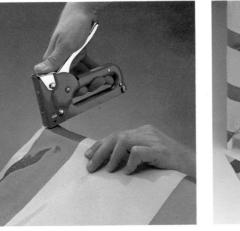

9 *Use tacks or staples to secure awning material. Fix first at centre of frame and move outwards to prevent creasing*

10 *Overlap the gussets so that water cannot seep through between them, then tack or staple them in position*

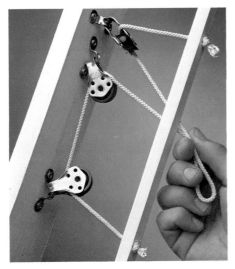

12 *This photograph shows how the single pulley system works. There are many different types of pulley*

13 *A stout cleat screwed to the wall is enough to secure the pulley rope whether the awning is up or down*

becomes a serious problem at the sides where you must cut the triangular gussets. To counter this problem, buy some plastic or cloth tape—even webbing will do—and lay it over the cut edge of the material before you tack it.

Make sure the tape slightly overlaps the cut edge, and tack it down in the same way as the rest of the material. If you find that the material continues to fray, then untack it, stretch it over the frame and sew a hem on to it. This has the added advantage that it strengthens the material.

The simplest solution, of course, is to choose a rubberized material.

Finishing the awning

Leave yourself enough rope to run, when the awning is open, from the lowest frame to the pulleys, then to the cleat and back to the other pulley, finally ending at the second securing point on the lowest frame.

Now feed one end through one pulley on the double block to the other pulley and then through the hole drilled in the lowest frame. Double knot the rope on the other side, or double it round the frame and tie to the rope as it enters the frame.

Feed the other end of the rope through the spare pulley on the double block and secure, as above, to the lowest frame at the opposite hole. Finish tacking the material on the lowest frame into place around the holes for the rope. Fig. 12 shows how the pulley arrangement should look.

The bottom edge of the awning will look best if it is finished with a matching scalloped or fringed trim. Otherwise, just buy a length of heavy fringing from a soft furnishing supplier. The trim should be put on the lowest frame and tacked in place with a plastic trim over the material.

Now check that the whole system works smoothly and does not snag or catch as the awning is raised and lowered. Apply a small amount of light oil to the hinges, pulleys and pulley swivels. Fix a stout cleat to the wall to wind on the pulley rope when the awning is raised or lowered (fig. 13). Finally, give all screws a fractional turn to ensure they are fully tightened.

Properly made, the awning should not tear or suffer undue damage. But storms and high winds can cause problems such as rips and holes. To repair them, take the awning off the wall and try to stitch the material back together. You may find it easier to iron, sew or glue a matching patch.

If a frame member breaks you may have to remove the material to repair it.

CHAPTER 3

PATHS

Brick is an extremely versatile and durable material that can be used not just for building walls but for creating decorative surfaces for paths, patios, drives—even flights of garden steps. Easy to lay and available in myriad colours and a selection of textures, brick pavers (and their moulded concrete block counterparts) offer enormous potential for designing pathways through your plot.

LAY A BRICK PATH

The attractive appearance of brickwork need not just be confined to house building and boundary walls—paths, drives, patios and steps all look great built in brick.

The porous nature of some ordinary bricks makes them unsuitable for paving work. Coming into direct contact with the ground, with no protection against damp, they would quickly become saturated and start to crumble. For this reason you must use either engineering bricks, purpose-made paving bricks or concrete block pavers. They're available in many different forms, all of which are extremely dense and hard—making them impervious to moisture and frost.

Paving bricks and blocks vary in size from about 215×65mm×33mm to 215mm×215mm×35mm and come in a variety of colours. They are not as deep as ordinary bricks, and this saves time and effort when digging the trench for the path.

Best of all are the rough stock bricks which are kiln-burnt longer than other types, giving them a very red appearance and making them more resistant to bad weather conditions.

Alternatively, you might like to consider using old bricks bought from a demolition contractor: if they have withstood 50 years or more without crumbling (in the same sort of situation that they are to be used in now) they are bound to be resistant to frost and moisture—and they may be cheaper than new bricks.

Remove the old mortar on the bricks with a chisel and hammer. You can use the old mortar as hardcore for the foundations.

Brick patterns

Brick paths, drives and patios can be laid in a variety of patterns (fig. A)—basket-weave, herringbone and running bond are popular examples.

Running bond (bricks laid end-to-end and joints staggered from row-to-row) is easy and quick to lay; it's exactly the same as the stretcher bond used for walls, and the bricks can go either across the path or lengthways.

You can make the patterns even more attractive by varying the colours of the

Right: *Laying a brick path is a very straightforward task but the finished result looks attractive and is very hard-wearing*

bricks. For instance, in basket-weave bond, you could have one half red and the other in a very pale colour to give a chess board effect or a diagonal pattern. Use a simple run of bricks to form the borders, with either the stretcher (side) or the header (end) faces butting up the edges of the path.

For a more varied appearance you can lay a ragged brick edging, as shown in fig. A, though this uses more bricks than the simpler bonding methods. For wide areas —such as a patio or drive—it is a good idea to start by paving one or two longitudinal

---

★ WATCH POINT ★

Where a path is to curve, fix one peg to the middle of the site and attach a length of twine as long as you want the furthest part of the curve to extend (fig. B). Stretch this taut to another peg, level it, then move the second peg around as a compass as you dig out the foundations. Shorten the twine, and repeat for the inside edge of the path.

---

courses each side to act as a gutter and border.

You can also obtain some interesting effects by laying bricks on edge, although this method uses a lot more bricks and is consequently more expensive.

Preparing the site

Before starting to lay any foundations drive in pegs at each corner of the proposed path. Stretch twine taut between them, check this for level by holding a spirit level on top, then adjust the height of the pegs where necessary so that you have a level guide for the foundations (fig. 1).

A patio or path is not usually expected to take great weight, so most ground can be made to suit the job. If the soil is very firm, try not to disturb it when marking out the area—simply pull out any grass or weeds, fill any hollows and roll the surface flat (fig. 2).

If the ground is soft, you must lay down a layer of rubble or stones, compact it with a roller then cover it with a layer of sand to fill in any voids. You will need to remove

1 *Mark out the path with twine stretched between pegs. Adjust the twine with the help of a spirit level to obtain the right slope*

2 *If you are laying the path on firm ground fill any holes and take away bumps, then roll it smooth with a heavy roller*

3 *To make a sand foundation spread the sand over the site and then smooth it down so that it is about 50mm deep all over*

4 *Now lay the bricks down in the desired pattern, spacing them about 15mm apart and removing or adding sand to make them level*

5 *Protecting the bricks with a piece of wood, tap them with a heavy club hammer to make the surface as level as possible*

6 *Spread sand over the path and brush it well into the cracks, leaving a trough of about 30mm deep between the bricks*

some extra soil to allow this.

Where soft patches occur in otherwise firm ground, fill them with rubble, compact it well and roll it level. In extremely wet conditions, or where the site is below surrounding ground level, it is a good idea also to install a 25mm wide sub-soil drain in a bed of clinker beneath the hardcore. If possible, the drain should have a slight gradient and discharge into a soakaway (a rubble-filled pit, which filters the water away). However, it is a good idea to consult your local building inspector at the planning stage if this is necessary.

Ideally, all paths should have a gradient of 25mm in one metre to ensure rapid drainage of rainwater. To obtain this, check that the marking-out pegs are level then adjust their heights so that the twine between them slopes right away from the house. As you use the twine as a guide for digging the foundations, the gradient will eventually be transferred automatically to the bricks themselves.

7 *Finally spread a dry mortar mix over the path, brush it into the joints then sprinkle with water using a watering can with a fine rose*

A gradient of 25mm every three metres is sufficient for a level patio, but a site which slopes dramatically away from the house also needs a soakaway at the far end—a shallow, gravel-filled trench will do the job.

When the patio site slopes heavily towards the house, bring the adjoining edge

★ WATCH POINT ★

A paved patio which butts up to the house must be at least 150mm below the level of the damp proof course (DPC) so that rainwater cannot splash up to the wall above it and so cause a damp problem indoors. For the same reason water should not be allowed to collect where the patio joins the house.

up to ground level with hardcore and insert a vertical DPC against the wall of the house. This can be a strip of bituminous felt.

Bedding material

The site for paths and patios needs to be excavated to about 100 to 150mm, depending on which bricks you use. Though bricks can be laid directly on to a well-tamped bed of clay or gravel, the path is best protected against subsidence by laying a sub-foundation of concrete. Make the concrete bed from one part cement to six parts all-in ballast and with just enough water to make the mix workable.

Lay the concrete to a depth of between 50mm and 75mm and set up formwork of timber planks on edge, nailed to wooden pegs driven into the ground outside the area of the path, to mould and retain the wet mix until it's hard. The surface need only be roughly levelled at this stage, as the mortar in which the bricks are laid will help to take up any irregularity.

Hardcore is not really necessary for paths and patios, but is for sites where the subsoil is soft. At least 100mm thickness of broken bricks or concrete should be laid—plus a layer of small chippings or stone dust and sand as the final layer. Alternatively, over the hardcore, 100 to 150mm of weak concrete can be laid, made up as described above.

Laying bricks on sand

Where the ground is naturally hard, a brick path can be laid loose on a bed of sand (fig. 3)—although you may have to excavate to a depth of 180mm before you reach sufficiently firm and level subsoil. In this case level off as much as possible, roll out the area, then spread a layer of sand over the site.

Lay down the bricks in the desired pattern, spacing them about 15mm apart and removing or adding sand as is necessary to get them to the required level (fig. 4).

You can compact the bricks into the sand bed by laying a stout length of wood over the rows in a manageable area, and tapping with a club hammer (fig. 5). This is fine for small areas but for a larger surface you'd be wise to hire a plate compactor: this machine, fitted with a rubber sole plate, will vibrate the bricks quickly and evenly into a

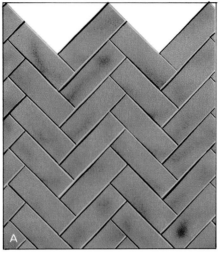

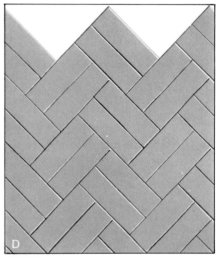
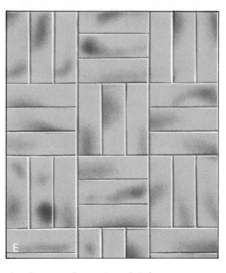
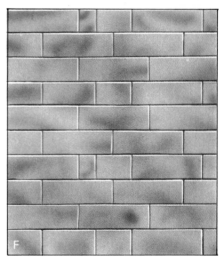

A. *Among the various brick patterns you can lay are (A) single herringbone bond (B) raking bond (C) diagonal basketweave (D) double herringbone bond (E) basketweave bond and (F) a mix of half bond and Flemish bond. You should bear in mind that the more complicated patterns will require some brick cutting* *which is both difficult and wasteful of material not to mention expensive. It should not be attempted if you do not feel confident enough to complete the job in a professional manner. If this is the case it is better to attempt only the easy patterns or you will only be disappointed with the result*

firm, level surface.

When you have laid all the bricks, spread sand over the surface and brush it well into the cracks (fig. 6). Pass over the surface once more—using club hammer and wood block, or plate compactor—to firm up the joints properly.

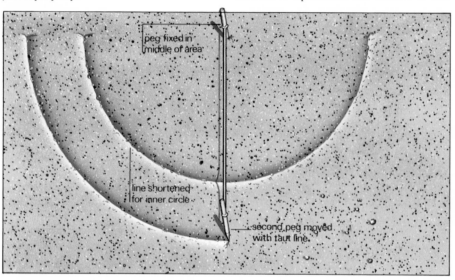

B. *To mark out a curved path, scratch the lines with this makeshift compass. Simply shorten the line to mark the inner edge*

Laying bricks on mortar

Before you start to lay the bricks, prepare two lengths of board, about 2m long × 125mm wide, and prop these at the side of the path as the bricks are being laid. Move the boards along as you work and lay a straightedge, with a spirit level on top, across them to act as a gauge to keep the surface level.

Use a guideline stretched taut along the length of the site to indicate their correct height; place this to the right if you are right-handed and to the left if you are left-handed.

Start at the lowest point of the proposed path and lay the bricks by pressing them into the mortar bed and tapping them gently into position with the handle of your club hammer until they're level: check this by holding a straight-edged length of wood

over them. It will help you to have a scale plan of your chosen design handy so that there can be no confusion over the pattern.

Brick borders

Adding a border to a brick path or patio serves three purposes—it makes the work look more attractive, helps to hold the bricks together and prevents grass and weeds from encroaching on the path.

Always use new, purpose-made bricks—soil piled up against them will make them more vulnerable to decay.

Another sensible precaution is to build the mortar up around the outside of the border bricks, as far as you can without ruining the appearance of the path. A raised border of, say, two courses would give even more protection. Lay these in the normal way, adhering to a recognized bond.

Brick steps

All the bricks suitable for paths are equally suitable for steps, although you must be careful to choose a type that does not become slippery when wet and therefore dangerous.

Before deciding how many steps to make, determine the height and horizontal width of the slope or incline by banging in a post—at least as high as the ground you are measuring—at the foot of the slope. Use another piece of wood to run from this to the level ground right at the top of the slope (fig. C).

When you have checked that the horizontal piece is level, measure exactly the height at which the posts meet. Measure the horizontal distance between them as well, then divide the proposed number of steps into this measurement to give you the width of the treads.

Before finally deciding on the number of steps, consider your proposed number in relation to the gradient of the slope: if it is steep, the riser should not be too high and the tread should be as wide as possible—at least 300mm.

Normally, it is possible to divide the height equally into steps with risers of about 100mm. But if this leaves too narrow a tread, reduce the height of the risers slightly.

The next stage is to roughly cut out the shape and number of steps and dig a trench to form the footing of the first riser. Continue this trench around the sides of the steps in preparation for the building of the side walls.

Next, excavate the steps to allow for a riser equivalent to the depth of two courses of the bricks you are using plus a 50mm mortar bed and two 15mm mortar joints. Excavate gradually, checking for level all the time.

When you are satisfied that the steps have been correctly cut and are level, fill in the trench with a 1:5 mix of cement and all-in ballast. When this is set—and it will probably take at least a day—the first riser and tread can be laid. For this, you need a mortar mix of 1:3 cement and builders' sand. Lay the first course of bricks for the riser in a stretcher bond on a 50mm bed of mortar and lay the next course on a 15mm bed.

For laying the front course of the tread, single bull-nose bricks are satisfactory, although for comfort and safety the nosing should be of a small radius. If you use conventionally shaped bricks, adjust the level of the mortar to allow for a slight drainage gradient and also to stop water gathering.

Lay the front course flush with the second course of the riser and complete the tread in the normal stretcher bond. Carry on this way until all the steps are complete, remembering to check each course for level before moving on to the next. Fig. C shows how the entire flight of steps can be made.

To prevent subsidence of the soil from the steps and to give them a more attractive appearance, you should now build a side wall. Check that the ground is level before you begin, then build the wall in a stretcher bond using the same bricks for uniformity.

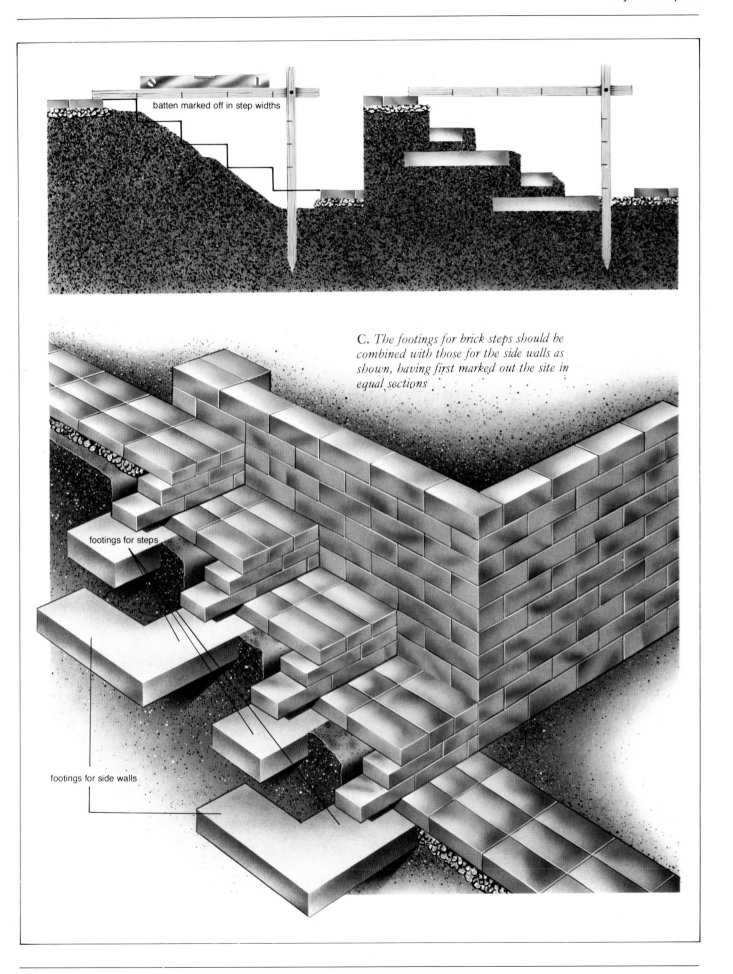

batten marked off in step widths

C. *The footings for brick steps should be combined with those for the side walls as shown, having first marked out the site in equal sections*

footings for steps

footings for side walls

DECORATIVE PAVING

Pathways are often left until last in the overall design of a garden. They end up as functional elements of the design rather than the decorative accents they could so easily become—with a little thought and planning.

Your garden path need not be a simple strip of concrete. By using unusual materials which blend in naturally with the surroundings, you can create a pathway which is an attractive feature of the garden and is not purely a functional necessity.

Using bricks

Bricks are a natural alternative to concrete, being both easy to lay and very durable, as described in the last section.

Available as special paving bricks or simply as regular building site material—such as hard engineering bricks—bricks come in so many colours and textures that they can blend in with any type of garden.

For instance, patterned red paving bricks provide a subtle contrast to predominantly green and woody shrubs and plants. Just imagine what a simple concrete path would have looked like. The natural texture and warmth of the red bricks adds significantly to the overall atmosphere of the garden. They are by no means a material for just another path!

Similarly a path laid with neutral coloured bricks sets off and enhances the bright flowers which line its length.

In this case bright red bricks would have been distracting. These bricks have been laid in mortar but most paving bricks can be laid simply on a bed of sand that has been well tamped down and compressed.

Paving stones

Unlike brick, paving stones are usually fairly neutral or pastel coloured and to make the most of their special appeal they should be laid out in interesting and different patterns.

They are the ideal paving materials for small gardens and patios and if they are laid as in the picture they can allow quite a bit of greenery to spill over into any confined space. Using grass as a filler between staggered slabs is a particularly effective way of breaking up what might otherwise be a cold expanse of grey across the width of the patio.

The path pictured across the lush green lawn could have been laid simply as a straight line with parallel sides; but how much better to stagger the pattern in semi-geometric steps, giving the effect of a winding pathway without any elaborate curves.

Wooden paths

Usually, the first choice for paving material is some kind of stone, or other hard, rock-like covering. It is not generally realized that deep wooden beams can be just as effective. They are even simpler to lay than bricks—the best kind of wood to use being scrap or driftwood, which is cheap and easily obtainable.

★ WATCH POINT ★

As long as the wooden beams are thoroughly soaked in preservative before they are laid, a properly designed wooden pathway can take many years of wear.

But the ideal bedding material for a wooden walkway is a spread of gravel or small pebbles as illustrated.

Well-seasoned old wooden beams can be embedded in such material either by digging deep grooves in an existing sweep of stones or by laying the wood on the bare ground and then infilling with carefully graded pebbles to pack down the beams tightly against each other. Vary the lengths of each slat to get a ragged edge to the

Left: *Red paving bricks can add a subtle and attractive contrast to a very green-looking garden*

according to size and colour can be bought from specialist garden centres and sometimes from builders' suppliers. If you have the patience, a mosaic path made from finely graded pebbles can look very attractive and almost Mediterranean in style.

A rough stone path is not as easy to lay as it might at first appear. The stones are readily available from quarries and suppliers of rubble and hardcore, but you must choose each stone very carefully, looking for the ones with flat surfaces which can

★ WATCH POINT ★

The small pebbles should be embedded in a screed of wet concrete and it is important to choose each stone carefully—setting it against its neighbours so that an even surface is produced overall.

Left: *Rough stone paths are not that easy to lay. The stones must have level surfaces and butt together easily*

Below: *Wooden beams laid crossways can make an unusual-looking path but they need to be kept moss-free*

path and add that characteristically rustic, weathered look.

The pathway which has a bed of stones on one side and a lawn on the other provides a natural link between two different areas of activity in the garden.

The beams have been laid lengthways to create a tidier effect than those laid crosswise and a series of wooden steps links this section of the path to a conventional concrete type around the edge of the lawn.

Wooden paths age very differently from the brick or concrete varieties, developing a thin covering of moss and lichen. Although this can often add to their charm, such growths should be cleared from the actual trodden part of the path as they can be slippery in wet weather. Mossy borders, on the other hand, look delightful.

Pebbles and mosaics

Beds of pebbles are an easy way to cover large areas of ground where plants will not grow, because the ground is shady or otherwise unsuitable. Pebbles graded

then be laid uppermost.

Properly laid rough stone paths look very attractive and are particularly suited for gardens full of bushes and trees. They have an old-fashioned, country feel and lend an air of age and maturity to any garden, however small. Part of their charm is the weeds and plants that sprout up in the cracks, but again such growths are best cut back every so often or they will engulf the whole path and become a safety hazard in damp and wet weather.

Above: *An attractive geometric pattern of paving stones can really be the highlight of a rather plain garden*

Choosing your paving

If you are thinking of relaying one of your garden paths or even laying a completely new one, consider the various areas of the garden through which it will run.

There is no strict rule that says the nature of the path must be the same along its whole length. You can use one or more of the ideas discussed here to blend in the path with the surrounding aspects of the garden.

Above: *Paving stones can be laid with a large space to let grass grow in between them for variety of colour*

Left: *Wooden beams can also be laid lengthwise for a neater, and more uniform, path in the garden*

CHAPTER 4

FENCES

Fencing is both utilitarian and decorative. Whether it's used to define the boundaries of your property, or simply to enhance or separate different parts of the garden, you'll find there's a wide range of types available. Close-boarded fencing is one of the most popular styles: it's not only durable and attractive but also adaptable in use and straightforward to construct. More practical, but a cheaper alternative that's the ideal choice for keeping things in or out, chain link fencing offers easy erection and a largely maintenance-free structure.

A CLOSE-BOARDED FENCE

A garden fence built from overlapped vertical boarding is an attractive addition to any home. Close-boarded fencing—as it is called—is not difficult to build and uses pre-cut timber, making it a realistic alternative to the cheaper but less durable 'woven panel' fencing.

Three things make all the difference between a shoddy fence and an attractive, solid, long-lasting one. First and foremost the posts must be adequately supported. Many people try to save money by skimping on the length of the posts or the amount of concrete used to bed them, but this is false economy, as the first gale may quickly demonstrate.

Also, the timber must be adequately protected against rotting. Although fencing timber is sometimes sold pre-treated against rot, it pays to give it the extra protection of a good soaking in preservative before erection. Additionally, all cut ends and

every joint must be well soaked in pre-servative before they become inaccessible.

Finally, the fence should be straight and its post tops level or, if on sloping ground, descending in steps of equal sizes. If your land slopes, you need to work out in advance whether to have a sloping or stepped fence, and whether you will use gravel boards or a plinth beneath it.

Construction materials

Though oak is the traditional fencing material, purpose-cut, low grade softwood is used in preference nowadays because of its lower cost. This can be perfectly acceptable provided the timber is properly treated with

Below: *Building a timber fence like this is surprisingly easy, providing you tackle the work in a logical order*

preservative. The posts are of 75mm × 75mm sawn timber—sometimes available as prepared 'fencing posts'—which are sunk at least 600mm into the ground and sleeved in concrete. Two or three arris rails—depending on the height of the fence—fit into mortises in the posts. The rails are triangular in section; usually 100mm on one side, 75mm on the other two.

The vertical boards are feather-edged softwood, 100mm wide and tapering from 20mm at one edge to about 6mm at the other. When erected, they are overlapped by about 25mm.

To prevent the bases of the boards rotting, a horizontal gravel board is fixed between the posts just above ground level. Lengths of 100mm × 25mm timber are suitable, and should be fixed to 38mm × 38mm wooden cleats. As an alternative, you can use a masonry

plinth—a dwarf wall—of either bricks or concrete walling stones set on a concrete pad.

You can make your fence even more durable by fixing capping pieces and a weathering strip.

Fig. C clearly shows the full constructional details for putting up a close-boarded fence.

Preservation

Fencing timber is particularly susceptible to rotting, especially the softwood type. The most vulnerable area is the 100mm or so at, and immediately below, ground level; sometimes this will rot through, leaving the wood above and below it more or less intact. This is why it pays to carry your supporting concrete at least 50mm above ground level and give it a finishing 'crown' to run off the water.

If you cannot get pre-treated timber, treat the wood yourself by soaking it in a bath of exterior timber preservative. To make the

★ WATCH POINT ★

Pressure or vacuum-impregnated timber (such as the Tanalised variety) is best for fencing but is expensive and sometimes difficult to obtain from timber merchants.

bath you need about two dozen old bricks and a 3m wide sheet of heavy-duty polythene (fig. A).

Find a suitable flat surface and arrange the bricks on edge to form a rectangle—slightly longer than the largest fencing post and wide enough to take all the timber. Lay the polythene over the bricks to form a bath then carefully pour in the preservative, taking care not to cut or otherwise puncture the sheeting. Steep the fencing materials for up to a week, if possible. Cover the bath during this time if children and pets are around.

If you have to store timber out of doors for any length of time, lay it on a flat surface and cover to prevent warping. Leave plenty of ventilation space between individual boards.

As you erect the fence, paint preservative on all timber surfaces that you will not be able to reach later—for example, where the vertical boards overlap each other. Give all the fence's end grain an extra coat to protect it thoroughly.

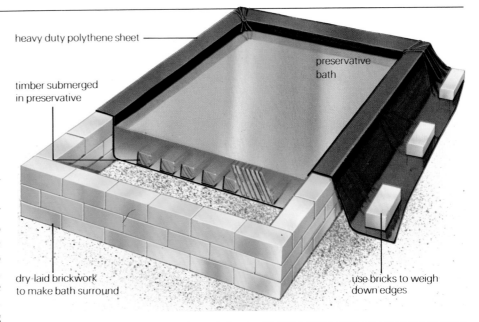

A. *If you are building an entire fence, it is well worth constructing a bath for timber preservative. Leave timbers to soak as long as possible*

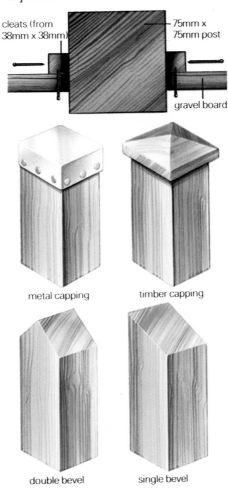

B. *Gravel boards are secured to fence posts with hardwood cleats (top). Protect the tops of fence posts using one of these methods*

Initial preparation

Begin by using a line and pegs to set out a straight line for your fence. Nylon fishing line is best for this, and especially for some of the levelling you may need to do later, as it does not sag when damp.

Decide how far apart your posts are to be—but to save cutting, base this on the length of the arris rails. If your arris rails are 2440mm long, set the posts 2440mm apart, measuring from the centre (not the outside edge) of one post position to the centre of the next. If this means that one fencing panel must be narrower than the others, arrange for it to be at the least conspicuous end, or corner, of the run of fencing.

Next, prepare your posts. The mortises are cut to take 100mm × 75mm × 75mm arris rails. Mark out slots 75mm high × 25mm wide, inset 20mm from the face of the post.

For a fence on level ground, begin the upper mortise 250mm from the fence top, and the lower one 300mm above ground level—that is, 900mm from the bottom of the post if this is bedded to a depth of 600mm.

If the fence is to be more than 1200mm high, add an extra mortise at the mid-point to accept the third arris rail which is necessary to strengthen the construction. Mark out the mortise positions with a try square and pencil, drill from both sides with a brace and 25mm bit (fig. 1), and use a 19mm or 25mm mortise chisel to square the holes neatly.

If you do not intend to use post caps, cut the top of each post so that it slopes away at 45° on the side on which you will be fixing

1 *Start cutting the mortises for the arris rails by drilling two or three large holes. Afterwards, finish off with a mortise chisel*

2 *Even if the fencing timber is already coated with preservative, you should apply more of the compound to all the exposed cut areas*

3 *Use a small axe to trim the ends of the arris rails roughly to shape. You can use a saw instead, but this does take longer*

★ WATCH POINT ★

For a stepped fence on sloping ground the mortises on the 'uphill' and 'downhill' sides of the post will have to be offset, and cut only halfway through the post.

---

the boards. This ensures that rainwater runs off the vulnerable end grain.

Next, using a small hand axe, taper the ends of the arris rails enough for them to jam into their respective mortises (fig. 3). For a level fitting, try to leave the face of the longest side intact and cut instead into the top edge, bottom edge and back. Check the fit of the arris rails in the mortises (fig. 4): an exact fit is not necessary, but the neater you are the easier the assembly becomes. Remember to dab preservative around the insides of the mortises and the cut ends of the rail (fig. 5). Also, try to make all the cut ends of the arris rails of equal length—this greatly enhances the overall appearance of the fence.

Making the post holes

Once you have checked that your rails go halfway through the posts—and that your proposed post spacing is therefore accurate—you can mark the positions of the post holes.

Post holes need to be wide enough to allow for a decent sheath of concrete around the posts, but not so wide that they waste material. A narrow hole 600mm deep is hard to dig with a spade; a better tool is a post hole borer—sometimes called a ground auger—available from a tool hire shop. To

use it, you just drive it in the ground like a corkscrew then withdraw it and the necessary earth.

Use the spade to trim the hole to about 200mm square. If you have the strength and the ground is soft enough, you may be able to 'pile drive' the post into its final bedding depth. You should then remove any loose material from the bottom of all the holes.

If you are planning to build a masonry

plinth, dig the footings at this stage.

Next prepare shuttering from scraps of timber or plywood so that you extend the concrete sleeve above ground level and so protect the post at its most vulnerable point. Quite how far you extend it depends on whether the fence is beside loose soil, gravel, or concrete, and whether you are using a plinth. Do not go too far or you may find it will be difficult to fix the cleats for the gravel boards.

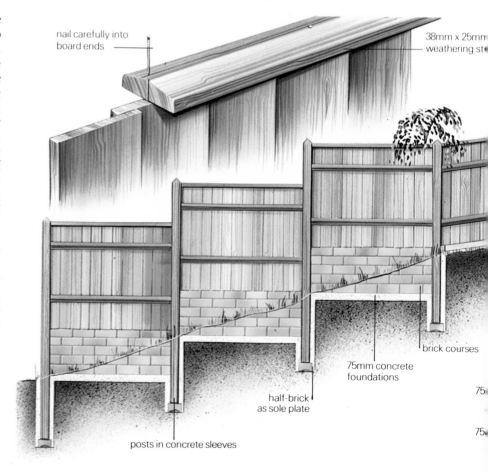

nail carefully into board ends

38mm x 25mm weathering st[...]

brick courses

75mm concrete foundations

half-brick as sole plate

posts in concrete sleeves

75[...]

75[...]

4 *Be sure to try each arris rail for fit in its mortise, otherwise you will run into difficulties during the assembly of the fence*

5 *Make certain that the cut ends of the arris rails get an extra coat of preservative, or they may become a focus for rot in the future*

6 *A line is used to mark the positions of the post holes. Check the fit of the post and rail before you start to assemble the fence*

Erecting the fence

When installing posts, ramming material around the base of a post loses much of its effect unless the bottom of the hole itself is really hard. So use a half brick or lump of concrete as a sole pad in each hole: this also ensures water drains away quickly.

Erecting fence posts is much easier if there are two people, because one can hold the post plumb while the other rams in the concrete.

But if you are alone, stand the first post upright, fit a timber brace on each side, then use a plumbline or spirit level to check that it is vertical. When it is, fix the other ends of the braces to pegs driven into the ground.

Use a concrete mix of one part cement to six of all-in ballast. Pour it into the hole a little at a time and ram it well down with the end of a length of timber (fig. 8), checking as you go that you are not knocking the post out of plumb. Slightly over-fill the shuttering with concrete, then use a trowel to slope it to a smooth finish like the flaunching around a chimney pot.

Leave the concrete to set enough to hold the first post firmly and stand the second post on its sole pad. Fit the first set of two (or three) arris rails between the two posts. Check that the post is plumb and that the top rail is level. You may be able to tap them

C. *Constructional details of a close-boarded fence. Note that where a slope is involved, you can either slope the panels to match or step them and use masonry plinths to provide a firm base*

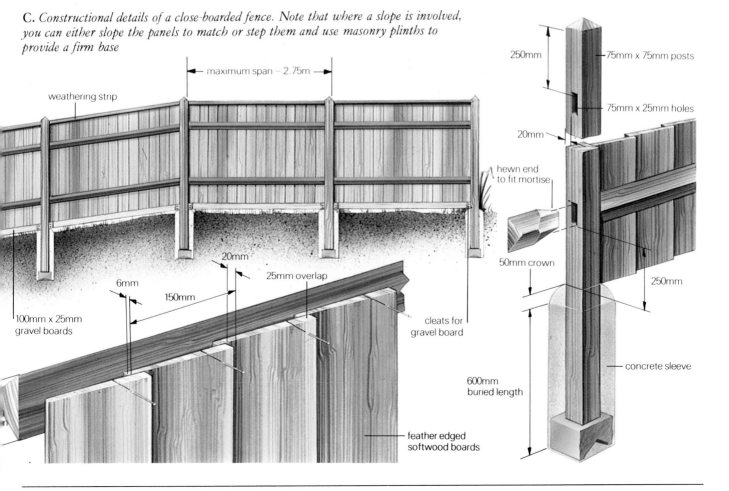

maximum span – 2.75m

weathering strip

250mm
75mm x 75mm posts
75mm x 25mm holes
20mm
hewn end to fit mortise
50mm crown
250mm

20mm
6mm
150mm
25mm overlap
100mm x 25mm gravel boards
cleats for gravel board
600mm buried length
feather edged softwood boards
concrete sleeve

into line gently (fig. 7): if not, scrape out more earth from the second post hole or pour a little concrete under the sole pad. Then pour just enough concrete to steady the second post while you check that it is properly vertical. When it is, pour, ram and trim off the rest of the concrete.

Continue in the same way until you come to the final section. Then measure off the last arris rails to the required length and erect your last post. Secure the arris rails to the posts by driving galvanized nails through the mortises into their tapered ends (fig. 9).

Installing gravel boards

The next stage is to install the gravel boards or build a plinth. Unless you are deliberately sloping the gravel boards, keep the top edges a constant distance from the tops of the posts. Doing so means you need only measure once—not several dozen times—when you come to cut the vertical boarding to length. Mark the height you want on a rod or an offcut of timber, measuring from the top downwards, and use this to gauge the height required on all posts.

Make the cleats to hold the gravel boards from 38mm × 38mm timber, the same length as the boards are wide. Inset them 25mm on the posts so that the faces of the gravel boards lie flush with the posts, and secure them with 65mm galvanized nails. Cut the gravel boards to length and nail them to the cleats (fig. 10). Ensure, in the future, that soil does not build up against them.

Close boardings

To keep the vertical boards level at the top of the fence, stretch a nylon line between the posts 25mm below their tops. Then cut a quantity of the feathered-edged boards to length.

Nail the first board in place, using 50mm galvanized nails, so that its thick end is against a post and the top is just brushing against the nylon guideline above.

Successive boards look neater if overlapped by a consistent amount, and although there is nothing to stop you gauging progress by eye, it is wiser to measure and mark on the arris rails the positions of the individual board edges (fig. 11). Alternatively you can use a measuring gauge for this. To make one, take a spare board and rule lines across it at intervals the width of your boards, less 25mm to allow

7 *Use a spirit level to check that the post is plumb as the first panel comes together. Hold the base of the post with pieces of hardcore*

8 *Once you have fixed shuttering around the post hole, ram in more hardcore then pour in the concrete and allow it to set hard*

10 *The gravel boards can be fixed as soon as the framework of the fence is complete. Nail them to cleats secured to the fence posts*

11 *Before you fix the vertical boarding, calculate the spacings needed to fill the panel then mark these on the arris rail*

13 *Once you have got started, use a wooden former to judge the overlap between boards: adjust this to save having to cut the last board*

14 *A panel of close-boarded fencing. The overall appearance is improved by regular spacings between boards and neatly cut rails*

9 *Secure the arris rails as shown, by nailing through the mortises in the fence posts. Use a club hammer to stop the post from jarring*

12 *Use a line, stretched taut between the first and last boards of a panel, to gauge the heights of the intervening boards*

15 *To weatherproof the tops of the fence posts, you can either cut them at a 45° angle or fit hardwood capping pieces as shown*

for the necessary overlap.

Tack-nail the board in place between the two posts, or lean it against the gravel board. Then line up each vertical board with the appropriate pencil mark as it is nailed firmly in place. Nail each board through its thicker end only, so that the nail just misses the overlapped board below it (fig. 13).

Try varying the overlap slightly in the later panels if it looks as though you must trim the final board. A variation of 3mm in the overlaps will not be noticed from one panel to the next but, over the width of a 2.5m panel, this can give you over 100mm of margin for adjustment—that is, plus or minus 50mm.

Fig. 14 shows how a completed panel should look, with regularly spaced boards and neat, horizontal rails.

Caps and weathering strip

Wooden capping pieces are useful for protecting the end grain on the tops of the posts, and are sometimes supplied with them. If not, you can make your own from 100mm × 25mm timber (as used for the gravel board), sawing it into 100mm squares. These are secured with galvanized nails (fig. 15).

Alternatively, fit metal caps over the exposed ends of the posts, nailing into the sides of the post.

The simplest way to weatherproof posts is to cut a double bevel or single chamfer at the top, so rainwater is shed rapidly. Fig. B shows typical examples.

Also useful is a weathering strip along the tops of the boards. You can make this by cutting 38mm × 25mm battens to length. Nail them on at the thick end of the board edges, carefully, to avoid splitting (fig. C).

Dealing with slopes

Whereas most other types of fence and, indeed, constructions of all kinds must be stepped on sloping ground, a vertically boarded fence can have a sloped top if the ground below it slopes only slightly. To maintain a consistent slope at the top of the fence, the procedure is to erect and plumb the highest post first, then temporarily erect the lowest post, plumb it, and hold it in position with cross braces. Stretch a nylon line between the two posts and use this as a height guide for the intermediate posts.

Otherwise proceed as for a level fence. Posts and boards must both be vertical. The

arris rails are sloped, but the slight step between successive boards which this creates is barely perceptible.

On steeply sloping ground it is still possible to slope the top of the fence, but a stepped top looks much better. Slightly longer posts are needed, however, and the first thing you need to know is by how much the ground falls away. It is no use trying to estimate this by eye, because ground falls are highly deceptive and usually greater than they look.

Start by temporarily erecting the highest and lowest posts. Sink them in the ground by only the usual 600mm and when plumb, use temporary braces to steady them.

Next, take a nylon line and fix it between the top of the lower post to an approximately level position, partway down the higher post. Measure the exact centre of the line and mark it with a dab of paint or tape. Then carefully level the line at the centre spot using a spirit level. Finally, measure the height from the line to the top of the higher post: this is the amount by which the ground falls between the two posts.

Now divide the total fall by the number of

★ WATCH POINT ★

At the bottom of a stepped fence like this, you must make some provision for following the slope of the ground, and you have a choice between sloping gravel boards or a masonry plinth.

panels—not posts—your fence will contain between the highest and lowest posts. If, for example, your fence is to have eight panels, and the ground slopes by 1850mm, you will want eight steps of about 230mm.

To achieve this, make the mortises on the 'uphill' side of each post at the normal level, as described above, and those on the 'downhill' side 230mm lower. (The first post, of course, has mortises only on its 'downhill' side, and the last post only on its 'uphill' side.) This means that, in this example, all the posts will need to be 230mm longer than standard.

Sloping gravel boards

On sloping ground, gravel board ends must be angled so that the boards follow the ground contour (fig. C). This calls for slightly longer gravel boards than would otherwise be necessary and you will need vertical boards of varying length, which rules out the use of a standard fence kit. The only alternatives are to use two or more gravel boards one above the other—which looks ugly—or build a masonry plinth.

To mark the gravel boards correctly, start by running a nylon line along the length of the fence and about 150mm above the ground. Lay each board against a pair of posts, aligning its top edge with the nylon line. Then use the posts themselves as marking guides while you scribe each board end to the correct length and angle. Number each board to ensure that it goes in the right place.

Fix the gravel boards to their cleats, as described, and then stretch a line across the post tops in the normal way. Stand each vertical board against the gravel board with the top just brushing the nylon line, then mark the correct length and angle. Use the spirit level to check the plumb of every other board.

Masonry plinths

A masonry plinth is almost as easy to construct as gravel boards are to fit, and certainly more durable. On sloping ground, it has the advantage that the top of each section can be level, so you do not need to scribe a lot of boards to varying lengths.

A plinth can be constructed of brick or walling stone. It is laid only between the fence posts (not continuously), and because it carries no weight, it needs only the lightest of foundations—concrete 75mm thick if the ground is reasonably firm (fig. C).

To build a plinth on anything but very level ground, you need to step the foot between post positions. Make the height of each step equal to one course of the building materials you choose to use, and the length a straight multiple of the brick or block length.

When you do this, do not forget to allow for a mortar bed between the foundation and the bottom course of masonry—and a double thickness of concrete where one step joins the next—or you will have nothing to bind the two steps together.

To avoid wasting material, cut the trench with a garden trowel or bricklayer's trowel —the average spade is too wide—and use the soil itself as shuttering. A couple of pegs driven into the bottom of each trench length and levelled with the spirit level will help to keep the foundation concrete level. An offcut of timber hammered into the ground can be used to retain the end of each step.

Above: *Making a dustbin screen can be an easy and straightforward project once you have learnt all the basic fencing skills*

If the soil is of a badly uneven consistency —topsoil patches, clay patches, rocky patches—and settlement seems likely, you can stabilize the wall by incorporating a length of galvanized expanded-metal wall reinforcement into the mortar joint between concrete and masonry.

While the concrete is hardening, stretch a nylon line across the fence posts above. Then, as you lay the masonry, use a gauge rod to keep each course at a constant height.

Making a dustbin screen

This practical dustbin screen will help to keep your garden neat and tidy. Simply build it as an extension to your close-boarded fence, using the techniques outlined in the preceding pages. You can easily adapt the basic design to the particular layout of your garden and also the access to it.

The first thing to decide is the most suitable location, taking into account where you need access to the dustbins and on which sides you want them screened. The drawings featured show four typical alternatives.

The screen is supported on one side by joining into one of the main fence posts, or in some cases, into two of them. When you are setting out the fence, you should take this into account, and site the posts accordingly. Cut extra mortises in these posts to take the arris rails for the screen. Stagger these to avoid weakening the timber unduly.

Set in the additional posts and fit the arris rails. Add the boarding, gravel boards and caps, treating all the timber with preservative. For a neat finish, you can pave over the enclosed area.

Making a dustbin screen

This simple dustbin screen is a useful addition to your fence. You can build it using the techniques and materials outlined on the previous pages. You may even be able to build it using left-over materials from the fence such as offcuts from the arris rails. You can build it to the same height as the fence as shown here, or economise on materials by building it lower, around 150mm taller than the bins

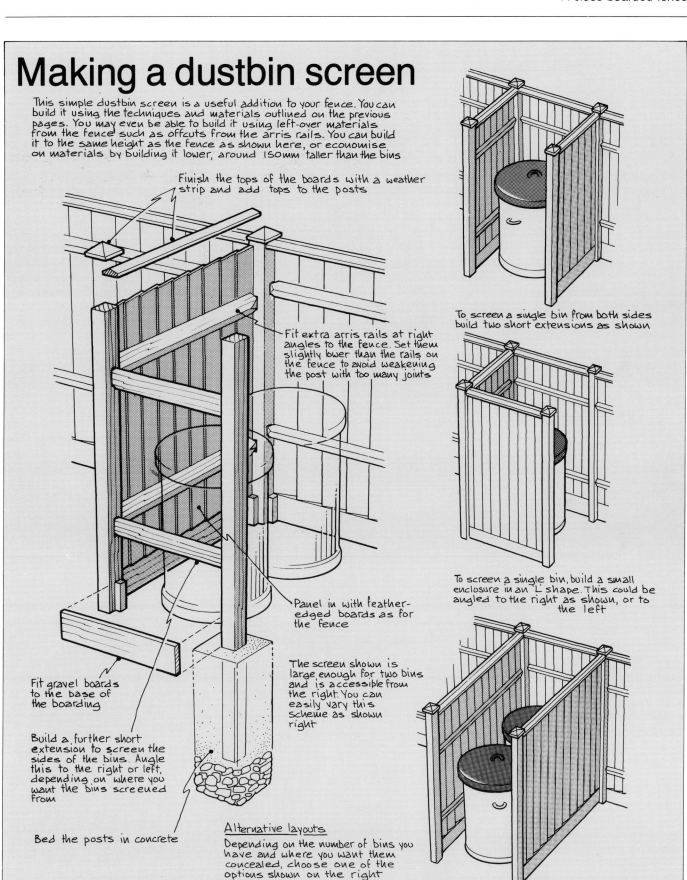

Finish the tops of the boards with a weather strip and add tops to the posts

Fit extra arris rails at right angles to the fence. Set them slightly lower than the rails on the fence to avoid weakening the post with too many joints

Panel in with feather-edged boards as for the fence

Fit gravel boards to the base of the boarding

Build a further short extension to screen the sides of the bins. Angle this to the right or left, depending on where you want the bins screened from

Bed the posts in concrete

The screen shown is large enough for two bins and is accessible from the right. You can easily vary this scheme as shown right

Alternative layouts

Depending on the number of bins you have and where you want them concealed, choose one of the options shown on the right

To screen a single bin from both sides build two short extensions as shown

To screen a single bin, build a small enclosure in an 'L' shape. This could be angled to the right as shown, or to the left

This arrangement will screen two bins from each side, leaving them accessible from the end

CHAIN LINK FENCING

Wherever you need utility fencing around the home, chain link systems offer the perfect compromise between low cost, long life and ease of erection.

As well as being cheaper than most other systems, chain link fencing is versatile, easy to put up, and good at its job of keeping things in—or out. But perhaps more importantly it is tough, durable and virtually maintenance free. Providing it is not maltreated, a chain link fence with steel or concrete posts should last as long as you need it.

Just about the only disadvantage of chain link is its utilitarian appearance. But where looks are important, there's no reason why you can't disguise the harsher aspects of such a fence by choosing coloured PVC-coated wire, painting the posts or training plants up the mesh, for example.

What's available

Chain link fencing comes in several different forms, although most of the systems work in more or less the same way (fig. A). A typical run has two end posts, called straining posts, which are set in the ground with their angled braces pointing in towards the line of the fence (fig. B). Between them, non-braced intermediate posts are set at intervals of 2.5m–3m. The actual chain link mesh is hung from tensioned straining wires running between the straining posts. Fences up to 1m high need only two of these wires—at top and bottom—but an extra middle wire is required for every 1m increase in height.

Mesh: The most commonly used mesh type is plain chain link, which comes in rolls corresponding to heights of between 900mm and 3600mm; lengths of roll vary, but 10m, 20m and 25m are usual. You normally have a choice of mesh size— 40mm, 45mm or 50mm are the most common—and wire gauge (2.0mm– 2.5mm is best for domestic use).

When it comes to finish, choose between plastic, galvanized and PVC-coated wire. Typical colours for the latter are green, bronze, white, black and grey. Coated mesh is generally no more expensive, is just as resistant to weathering and looks less utilitarian than the galvanized variety.

One up from plain chain link is decorative chain link, which may take many forms—the most popular style is the 'inter-

locking bow'. It is hung just like plain chain link and the choice in heights and finishes is much the same.

Welded chain link is a much stronger mesh which is normally reserved for high security fences, although decorative versions are also available. The thin gauges come in roll form (they are more difficult to work with than their plain counterparts) while the thicker gauges are sold as panels, the sizes of which can be made to order.

Posts: Here you have a choice between concrete, steel (galvanized, painted or PVC-

A. *There's a choice of mesh available: 1 is chain mesh. 2 and 4 are welded. 3 is light chicken wire. 5 is decorative mesh*

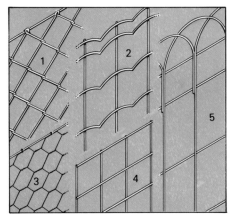

Below: Chain link fencing, although utilitarian in style, is very cheap to erect

coated), sawn wood and rough hewn hardwood stakes. Each type has its own advantages and a crucial bearing on the look of the fence.

Concrete posts can be found in several guises: as straining posts (the braces either bolt on or they're already attached), intermediate posts, double straining posts (to cope with changes in direction), corner posts (two braces at right-angles) and gate posts. They are pre-drilled to take straining wire fixings, mesh straining bars, hinge brackets and so on. The main advantages of concrete are its strength and weather resistance. Against this, however, concrete posts are heavy to transport and cumbersome, which generally restricts their use in domestic fencing to those below 2m high (although heights of up to 3.6m are widely available).

Steel posts, too, are strong and weather resistant. Their narrow section, which may be square, triangular, or L-shaped, makes them look flimsy on low fences but can be a definite advantage on taller constructions where concrete would look too heavy. The posts are usually pre-drilled to take different fixings; braces for straining posts bolt on and are sold separately. Steel straining posts must always be set in concrete but on firm ground the intermediate posts can simply be driven in with a sledge hammer—another advantage over concrete.

Sawn timber posts—generally in treated softwood, oak or cedar—have a softer, less

B. *Fixing methods for the straining wire and the stretcher bars vary from one type of post to another. Concrete and steel posts are pre-drilled to take the various matching fixtures, but wooden posts must be cut and drilled to suit fence height*

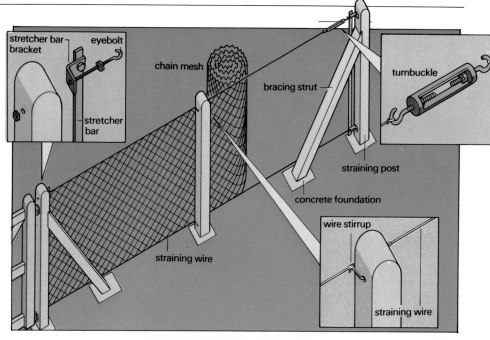

functional appearance but are liable to rot unless well treated with preservative. The straining posts will also have to be drilled to accept the eyebolts, and will have to be braced. Straining posts and braces must be set in concrete; intermediate posts can be driven into firm ground (fig. C).

Gates: Many manufacturers offer chain link gates as part of their ranges, but conventional close-boarded and ranch-style gates are usually just as easy to attach to the posts.

Hardware: This can vary between manufacturers, although it all works on the same principle. You're likely to need:

● Straining wire, which comes in 10m and 25m rolls, often with the fixings included.

● Straining bars—these are threaded vertically through either end of a run of mesh to straighten it. The bars are usually pulled against the straining posts and secured to angle brackets on the wire fixings.

● Wire fixings—at their simplest, for use with concrete or wooden posts and stakes, these are ordinary eyebolts which you fit through the posts and tighten to tension the wire. On some concrete post systems, the eyebolt is fixed and linked to the straining wire via a turnbuckle or bottle screw which can be altered to adjust the wire's tension. With metal posts, the fixing and tensioner are sometimes combined in a single unit called a tensioning bracket; this is bolted to the straining post.

● Intermediate fixings—to secure the straining wire, use wire staples on wooden posts and wire 'stirrups'—custom made from excess wire—on concrete and metal. The mesh is fastened to the straining wires every 150mm using wire 'S' hooks or short lengths of plain 3mm galvanized binding wire.

Planning the job

Assuming that you've chosen a style of fencing, the next thing to decide is the height. As regards the practical considerations, 900mm is perfectly adequate for boundary work, but you should raise this to 1200mm–1800mm for screening part of the garden, or 2750mm–3600mm for something like a tennis court. If you are concerned about

C. *Post holes are best made narrower at the top. Holes for braces are more difficult to estimate. Dig all holes at the same time, set upright posts first, then use braces to adjust the level of the brace post holes. Make sure that the posts are level and vertical*

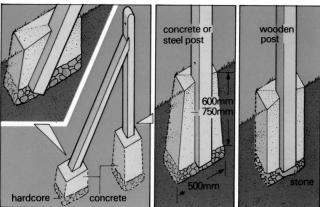

keeping burrowing pets in—or pests out—it's best to erect the fence in a shallow trench, in which case add 300mm to your chosen height.

When it comes to UK regulations, fences sometimes require planning permission. Normally they do not if:

● The fence is under 1m high along a boundary with a road.

● The fence is under 2m high along any other boundary of your property.

Unfortunately, local restrictions sometimes complicate the issue. You may, for example, live on a housing estate where

fence heights were restricted when the original planning permission was granted. Or your fence may constitute an obstruction to the view of drivers on the highway, even if it is on the borders of your property.

About the only way to be sure is by contacting your local authority planning office. It might also be wise, as a matter of common courtesy, to check with any neighbours whose property might be affected by the erection of the fence.

Buying the fencing: Before ordering, make a quick survey of the site. If this is sloping, there may be special considerations (see below). Otherwise, check that the ground is reasonably level along the length of the run and then measure it out.

Another useful tip is to check the soil and subsoil. Drive a stake into the ground at several places along the run to a depth of about 750mm: if you encounter many rocks it may be worth hiring a pick or pneumatic drill, although occasional obstructions can be circumvented by adjusting the post positions.

1 *Mark fence height on wooden posts; allow for the depth of the hole, the mesh height and an extra 100mm at the top*

2 *Drill 10mm holes for eyebolts at the mesh top and bottom lines. Make holes 10mm from front edge of posts*

6 *Cut the brace and the notch, then nail the two together. Pack the base with hardcore, then add the concrete*

7 *Lay out the fixing components—check you've ordered the right type and that you've got the right quantity*

The best place to buy chain link fencing is from a specialist supplier but always get more than one quote and don't forget to make the necessary delivery arrangements.
Other materials: As well as the fencing material and hardware, you need concrete and hardcore for bedding the posts. Buy the dry ingredients ready mixed for very small runs, otherwise use Portland cement and 20mm all-in ballast mixed in the ratio 1:5. You need hardcore too, but this can be any broken brick or stone that you happen to have lying around.
Tools for the job: Fitting the wires and mesh should require no more than a pair of adjustable spanners, screwdriver and pliers. Cutting 2.5mm gauge chain link can be done with pliers or pincers, though in most cases you don't need to—you simply unravel one of the interlocking strands (see below).

For sinking the posts, all you really need is a spade and spirit level plus a stringline and pegs; but if you've got a lot of holes to dig (or they're to be small and deep, for steel posts) then it's well worth hiring a post hole borer—a device which looks like a giant wood auger bit with a T-bar handle. Hire a sledge hammer for driving steel or hardwood stake intermediate posts. For wooden posts you'll also want a drill with 10mm bit; a saw, hammer and galvanized nails for securing the braces; and creosote or preservative to protect the timber.

Fixing the posts

This is the critical part of the job, so do it carefully. Above all, don't be tempted to skimp on the post hole depth or you may find that your work quickly comes crashing down.

Start by setting out the line of the fence using a stringline attached to pegs driven into the ground. The line must be level and taut—use enough pegs to stop it sagging—and you should set it about 150mm above ground level. Follow by clearing the site of all vegetation, roots and loose rocks, then mark on the line in chalk—or mark the ground with sand—where post holes will be needed.

Concrete posts

Holes for concrete posts must be a minimum of 600mm deep, increasing to 750mm for fences 1.8m high and 1m for those over 2.25m (your supplier should have taken this into account when you ordered the posts).

If you're digging with a spade, make the holes about 450mm square at the top and taper them out to 500mm square at the base. To use a post hole borer, position the tool at the centre of the proposed hole and put your weight on it while turning the T-bar clockwise—the auger should carve its way downwards with little trouble.

Exceptions to the depth rule are the holes you need to dig for the braces of the straining posts—these will work out roughly two-thirds as deep as the main post holes. Dig the main holes first, then hold the braces in place to gauge how much to dig out.

Position each post in its hole and wedge it with a brick or rock while you check the fence height mark against the line (don't forget to allow for the 50mm of hardcore). Remove the post and dig deeper or backfill as necessary, then shovel in 50mm of hardcore.

Replace the post and wedge it again or prop it with timber battening; use your spirit level to check that it is plumb and make sure that the fixing holes are pointing the right way.

Mix up your concrete with just enough water to bind the dry ingredients together—the mix should be slightly crumbly when squeezed in your hand. Shovel the concrete in around the post, compacting it as you go with a stout piece of wood. When you reach the top of the hole, level off and recheck the post for plumb: it should stay in position by

3 *Dig the post holes at your marks on the setting-out line. A post hole borer may prove worth hiring for heavy soil*

4 *Dig adjacent larger holes for the braces, then set all the upright posts in a mixture of concrete*

5 *When the concrete has cured around the upright posts, hold braces in place to mark cutting lines and housing joints*

8 *Fit eyebolts and stretcher bar brackets to each straining post—but don't tighten them up just yet*

9 *Attach straining wire to the eyebolts and then add turnbuckles if you need to make more adjustment*

or notch profile with it held against the post (fig. 5). Don't forget to soak all cut timber thoroughly with preservative before you nail the brace in place (fig. 6). Allow the post to project below the concrete.

When the concrete has cured, check the post for level—on all sides—and also check the lateral alignment of the posts. Shovel a few millimetres of soil over the concrete to disguise it.

Attaching the mesh

Although this is straightforward, the roll of mesh itself will be rather bulky and it may pay you to call in a helper.

Set out all the components to make sure everything's there (fig. 7). The first step is to fit the eyebolts—the straining wire fixings—to the straining posts. On most systems the eyebolts also hold the stretcher bar brackets, so don't forget to fit these, plus washers between every part. Leave the bolts—including the nuts that draw the brackets against the post—loose at this stage (fig. 8).

Take a roll of straining wire, thread it through the eye of the top bolt, and use a pair of pliers to turn it back on itself and twist it about seven times. Alternatively, if a turnbuckle is included, secure the wire to one end of this and fit the other end to the bolt (fig. 9). Leave the turnbuckle on an open 'loose' setting.

Run the wire to the far straining post, pull it taut, and cut it leaving a 150mm excess. Thread it through the eyebolt or turnbuckle and twist as before.

Now tension the wire by tightening the eyebolt nuts or turnbuckles at either end by equal amounts (fig. 10). Be careful when you do this: you don't want the wire to snap. As a rough guide, the tension is

itself, although you may need to prop a straining post until you've concreted the brace hole.

Leave the posts for at least three days, to give the concrete a chance to cure properly.

Steel posts

Holes for steel posts set in concrete can be smaller in diameter than those for concrete posts—say 225mm—but they must be at least as deep in relation to the height of the fence. Sink and station the posts in the same way, having first marked on the fence height, but use smaller pieces of hardcore so they don't sink through it.

Wooden posts

Wooden posts and stakes are best set in concrete, the hole sizes corresponding to those for concrete and steel posts respectively. Before you do so, however, the timber must be treated against rot.

Start by marking the fence height on each post, allowing for an extension of about 100mm at the top (fig. 1): this gives you the positions of the straining wire fixing holes, which you should drill using a 10mm bit (fig. 2).

Next give the posts a thorough coating of preservative, making sure that plenty of the fluid is allowed to drip into the drilled holes. As an added precaution, soak the bottom ends of the posts in a bath of preservative for a further 24 hours.

When you come to sink the posts, set the main strainer posts first (figs 3 and 4), let the concrete cure, then fit the braces and sink or drive in the intermediate posts—use setting-out lines *between* strainer posts for the correct alignment. Braces for stakes can simply be cut at an angle and then skew-nailed to the posts: right-angled offcuts at the bottom will make them more secure. But where sawn posts are concerned you'll make a neater job by sawing an angled housing joint out of the post.

Dig the hole for the brace first, then lay the brace in it and mark off the correct angle correct when kinks have straightened out and you start to feel appreciable resistance at the eyebolt nut.

Repeat this procedure for all the other straining wires in the run. Then secure them to the intermediate posts by threading further lengths of wire through the fixing holes and twisting the ends around the straining wires, or, with wooden posts, use wire staples to trap it against the posts.

Next take the free end of your roll of mesh and feed a stretcher bar through the end links. Bolt the bar to its brackets on the straining posts. Unwind the mesh along the straining wires—shaking it even as you go—and get your helper to fasten it temporarily to the top one with twists of wire (fig. 11). When you get to the other end of the run, feed another stretcher bar through the line of links that just reaches the straining posts.

Sever the mesh on the far side of the bar by untwisting the top link with a pair of pliers, unpicking the rest of the line, then untwisting the bottom link in the same way (fig. 12). This done, bolt the stretcher bar to its brackets on the straining post (fig. 13).

You should now be able to tension the mesh against the straining wires (and so complete the run of fence) by screwing in the nuts on the eyebolts which force the stretcher bar brackets against the posts. The only job remaining is then to secure the mesh to the straining wires every 150mm, using twists of wire as shown. If the mesh looks dishevelled and unevenly spaced, it's probably too loose. Remove the stretcher, unthread a strand, and move the bar in by one more strand, then repeat the procedure.

Dealing with sloping ground

Chain link fencing is flexible by nature, so minor changes in level rarely present any problems, providing you get the posts level and set the mesh just above the ground.

Where there are pronounced 'humps'—

10 *Tension the wire by tightening the eyebolt at either end or by making adjustments to the turnbuckles*

12 *At the other end of the fence, unravel a strand to cut the wire, then thread through a stretcher bar*

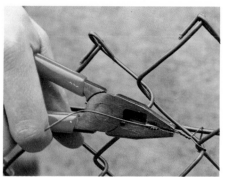

11 *Unroll the mesh from a stretcher bar fitted at one end and then loosely secure with wire twists*

13 *Secure the stretcher bars to their fixing brackets. Staple wire to the intermediate wooden posts*

your setting out line will show them up—it's worth levelling the ground first. The real difficulties occur, however, when there is a marked slope in one direction.

First of all, assess the scale of the problem: on a fairly gentle slope you can erect the fence as normal, with the posts

D. Deal with sloping sites by setting out a series of 'steps' in line with the gradient. At each change in level erect a two-way straining post. Drill four holes in each post for the straining wires. Erect intermediate supporting posts in the normal way

straight and the mesh angled between them; on a steeper slope you must 'step' the run into a series of terraces. The latter can involve excavation and levelling.

If you opt for steps, start by deciding how many you need and what length they should be. You can do this by measuring the total length of the run and then sketching it out on paper to see how much soil has to be removed.

When you've arrived at a reasonable compromise between length of terrace and excavation work involved, set out the site by driving in 450mm stakes at each step point and then erect levelled stringlines. This enables you to excavate each terrace more or less level using the line as a guide.

When you come to order the fencing materials, treat each terrace as a separate run with straining posts at either end. You will notice that not only must the intervening straining posts be 'double'; they must also be longer than is usual for the fence height by the height difference between steps, with two sets of straining wire fixing holes (fig. D).

In the case of concrete or steel posts, this can be arranged if you give your supplier a sketch plan of the terrace.

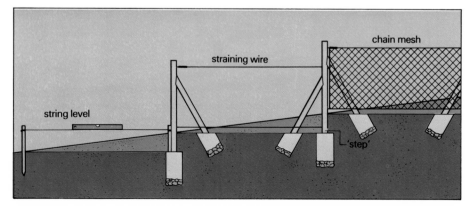

CHAPTER 5

OUTDOOR PLAY AREAS

Turn your garden into an adventure playground for your children with these fun-time projects, designed especially with safety and versatility in mind. To exercise growing limbs and a lively mind, there's a climbing frame that features swing, climbing rope, gangplank and other exciting accessories. For the younger members of the family there's a combined sandpit and paddling pool that brings the seaside to your back garden. The timber construction of both projects is simple, with no complicated carpentry joints to deter you.

KIDS' CLIMBING FRAME

There are two things which you can safely guarantee where children are concerned. One is their natural tendency to climb anything within reach and the other is the tedious regularity with which they fall over. The solution to this problem is to build a climbing frame which offers vital security and stability.

Half the fun of this climbing frame lies in its ability to change shape and cope with an array of bolt-on 'goodies' such as ladders, ropeways, swings and so on, which exercise the child's imagination as well as its body.

There are a number of essential factors to be considered with any climbing frame. It should never be too high for the child—two metres is a staggering altitude for a four-year-old but within reach of a child twice as old. Only you can determine, however, the parameters which best suit your own offspring—bearing in mind that children grow frighteningly fast. A climbing frame should also be sturdy, secure and should not offer any sharp edges or extensive protrusions which could cause an injury in a fall. And, of course, *supervision* is the final keystone to safety. Certainly no toddler should be allowed on a climbing frame unsupervised.

A demountable frame is an excellent choice. It can be stowed away during the winter months and simply erected for use when the sun comes out. For this reason a timber construction based on a modular principle is probably the most convenient and, comparatively, the least expensive. But before examining a typical construction, what are the alternatives?

Materials

It is tempting to use materials like scaffolding poles and clamps which you can cut to length. But this approach offers a number of hazards to the young climber. Sawn-through steel tubing, even if filed down, presents dangerous corners which, if not cutting young skin open in a fall, could cause serious grazes. The dangers are doubled if scaffolding clamps are used. In a swift descent back to earth, these could inflict serious injuries.

But not all forms of scaffolding are excluded and, in a number of cases,

Right: *This climbing frame can be great fun for young children and it is not difficult to construct*

products available on the market can serve purposes extra to the needs of children. Some scaffolding frames intended for DIY use represent a much safer alternative. Some types consist of open-frame steel panels about one metre wide by 600mm high. Each panel is self-supporting—in other words it is cross braced, rigid and secure. The panels simply slot together forming obstruction-free assemblies which, commonly, are used to construct tower platforms for exterior maintenance work.

While the height that these structures can reach is not recommended for junior members of the family, various low-level box structures can be easily erected to make an exciting and extensive climbing frame.

In some cases the frame components can be extended with short poles, curved interconnections and so on, to make portable garages or workshops over which tailor-made awnings fit for weather protection.

Such assemblies have a multitude of uses but—needless to say—they are not necessarily cheap.

Modular frames

The featured climbing frame is simple to make, inherently flexible in layout and, because only one type of standard component is used, can be extended to suit the funds available, the demands of the

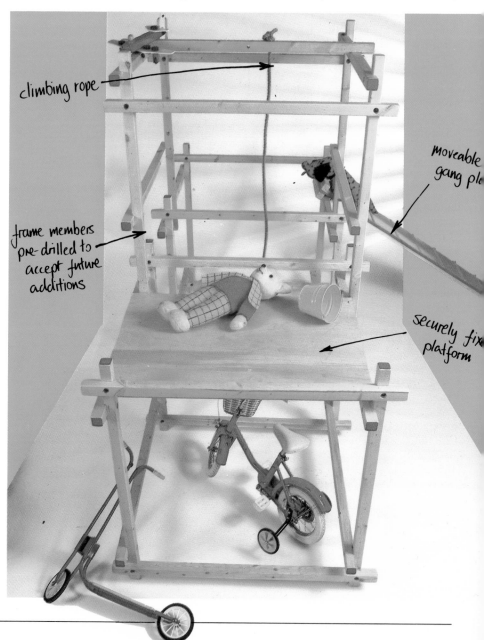

climbing rope

frame members pre-drilled to accept future additions

Moveable gang pl[...]

securely fix[...] platform

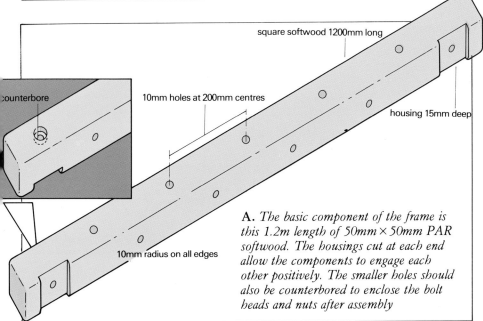

square softwood 1200mm long

counterbore

10mm holes at 200mm centres

housing 15mm deep

10mm radius on all edges

A. *The basic component of the frame is this 1.2m length of 50mm × 50mm PAR softwood. The housings cut at each end allow the components to engage each other positively. The smaller holes should also be counterbored to enclose the bolt heads and nuts after assembly*

50mm × 50mm PAR softwood and, for the 'rungs' on the gang plank, eight 300mm lengths of half-round ramin moulding.

To assemble the unit you use 70mm black iron coachbolts and nuts, each with a 10mm diameter shank. Use 110mm bolts with 75mm × 75mm timber.

To make the components you will need:
● a power drill with 10mm wood bit and a 25mm flat bit
● a cross-cut saw or jig saw and a tenon saw
● a tape measure, try square and steel rule
● medium- and fine-grade glasspaper
● screwdriver and 20mm No. 8 brass woodscrews
● a suitable socket wrench or box spanner
● paint or varnish, as you prefer
● a mitre box with right-angle slots.

Making the frames

The frame members are easily made, and when they are all complete you have broken the back of the job.

Start by cutting the timber into 1200mm lengths. Sand the cut ends and radius them slightly using a planer file followed by medium-grade glasspaper to remove any sharp edges (fig. 1). At the same time give all the edges a 10mm radius as well.

children, and the time available for manu-facture.

The basic component is a 1200mm length of 50mm × 50mm PAR (planed all round) softwood to reduce splinters, which has a wide housing cut in one of the surfaces at each end. Bolt holes drilled through adjacent sides along the length of the component allow you to bolt the pieces together in an infinite variety of com-binations, and to dismantle the assembly quickly and easily—either for storage during the winter or for some sort of change.

The dimensions given are a compromise between strength and cheapness; you could make the components from 75mm × 50mm timber, or even from 50mm × 25mm timber if you have a very young child, while you could equally easily reduce the length of the components to give a smaller overall size of frame. The choice is yours. However, if you intend to use the frame for access work around the house as mentioned earlier, you should choose timber of 75mm × 75mm cross section.

With the components assembled, you arrive at an open cube construction which is 1200mm along each edge. Two or three of these (or as many as you wish) form a large sturdy frame to which you can fix slides, swings and ladders.

Tools and materials

The featured design consists of three frames. To build this number you must buy 44m of 50mm × 50mm PAR softwood. Try to buy the timber in lengths which are multiples of 1.2m.

The two featured accessories are a 'gang plank'/slide, a simple swing and a platform. To build the platform you need a sheet of 19mm marine ply (for weather resistance) of 1.2m × 745mm. To build the slide you need a 2m × 300mm length of the same material. To make the end braces for the slide you need two 300mm lengths of

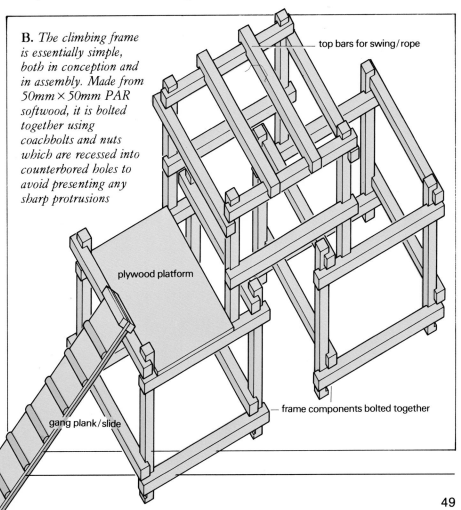

B. *The climbing frame is essentially simple, both in conception and in assembly. Made from 50mm × 50mm PAR softwood, it is bolted together using coachbolts and nuts which are recessed into counterbored holes to avoid presenting any sharp protrusions*

top bars for swing/rope

plywood platform

frame components bolted together

gang plank/slide

At each end of the same side you will need to cut out a housing 75mm wide by 15mm deep. Measure 40mm in from the end of the timber and, using a try square, mark a line across the width. Next measure 50mm along from that line and repeat the process (fig. 2).

Continue your pencil lines down both sides of the timber and mark a point 15mm down from the edge. Pencil this depth line in too. Secure the timber in a vice and, using a tenon saw and mitre box, cut down to the 15mm depth at each end of the housing, remembering to cut on the waste side of the pencil lines. Check as you do so that the saw is cutting evenly on both sides. Stop sawing just short of the bottom marks. Repeat the process across the width of the

housing at 10mm to 15mm spacings. This will make chiselling easier and prevent you from splitting the timber.

Gently mark the pencil lines at the bottom of the housing with your chisel, then start removing the timber from the top of the housing, working down and approaching from both sides. Ensure that your chisel stays horizontal to your work and finish off with light chisel strokes to smooth off the timber (fig. 3). Sand or rasp the bottom completely smooth, and repeat the process at the other end of the 1.2m length.

Using the 10mm twist bit, drill the bolt holes along the main frame. These should be spaced at 200mm intervals and alternate from top to bottom and side-to-side as shown in fig. A. Make sure that the holes are drilled at the exact centre of the timber face, and that your drill bit remains at right-angles to the surface.

Treat each frame section with a wood preservative before painting or varnishing it: make sure the compound can be over-painted when you buy.

Each of these frame components can now be bolted to one another, the housing helping to steady the structure. Add a washer under each nut, which should be

1 *Cut the frame members to the same length and radius the edges, first with a planer file, then with glasspaper to remove splinters*

2 *Mark the positions of the housings at each end of the components, and check that each one matches every other component*

3 *Cut the housings using a tenon saw and mitre box, then a wood chisel to shave the bottom of the housing to the correct depth*

4 *When drilling the bolt holes, start off by drilling a narrow pilot hole, then use the flat drill bit to drill the counterbores*

5 *When the counterbore has been drilled you can then enlarge the rest of the hole to the full 10mm diameter using an ordinary twist bit*

6 *Fit the components together, knock in the coach bolts using a ball-pein hammer and tighten the nuts using a socket or box spanner*

★ WATCH POINT ★

Before drilling the bolt holes through the housings, first drill a central pilot hole right through the wood using a 3mm twist bit. Reverse the timber and, using your pilot hole as a guide, drill down to a depth of 8mm using the 25mm flat bit (fig. 4). Then drill right through with the 10mm twist drill (fig. 5).

tightened with a socket or box spanner (fig. 6). Remember that if you use a frame section as a cross member as shown in fig. B the spacing between the housings must be matched by the gap between other frame members. This means, for example, that in a simple tower structure one of the horizontals secured between two uprights will be 'inside' the frame while its opposite number on the far side will be 'outside'. This won't affect the overall stability of the structure in the least.

Making the gang plank

A gang plank (fig. C) is easier to build than a ladder, as well as being cheaper and safer for the child. It can also double up as a slide, simply by turning it over.

Mark off a strip 2m long and 300mm wide on a sheet of 19mm marine ply, and mark the cutting lines with a sharp knife to break the surface ply and prevent splintering when you saw it. Cut the panel using either a panel saw or a power jig saw with either a saw fence or straightedge to guide the sole plate.

Sand down the cut edges but do not radius them at all. Using your try square mark pencil lines across the piece at 200mm intervals. To these lines fix 'rungs' from half-round sections of a hardwood such as ramin. Cut these to 300mm in length and drill three countersunk screw holes through their curved surfaces. Lay the rungs on the pencil lines and mark the positions of the screw holes in the top surface with a bradawl.

Fix the rungs down using pins and waterproof wood glue, and ensure that the heads are knocked well down (fig. 8).

At one end of the plank you must fix two 300mm timber battens, one on each side to form a grossly elongated 'T' shape. These battens will hook over the frame members to hold the plank securely in place whichever way up it is. Cut the battens from 50mm × 50mm PAR softwood and drill three counterbored screw holes 12mm deep along the length of each. As they will be on opposite sides of the same thin piece of timber, offset the holes slightly from one piece to the other so that the screws won't meet each other (fig. 9).

Fix the battens in place using waterproof

wood glue and 50mm No. 8 brass woodscrews, then sand them smooth. Don't radius their edges—this will only make them slip off the frame.

Adding accessories

There's no limit to a child's imagination, and it may take a little ingenuity to satisfy

an active, boisterous ten-year-old. Adding some simple accessories such as a swing, a climbing rope or a platform at the top of the gang plank can make the frame even more fun to play with.

Because of the bolt holes drilled through the main frame members you can fix accessories like swings or climbing ropes almost anywhere within the bounds of

7 *When marking cutting lines for either the slide or the platform, use a sharp knife to prevent the cut edges from splintering*

8 *Pin and glue the gang plank rungs in place and be careful to punch the pin heads well down before filling their holes*

10 *Screw down the slide's side rails flush with the edges to cover any splinters and fill the counterbored screw holes*

safety and common sense. The simplest swing consists of an old car tyre (thoroughly cleaned of rubber deposits and road grime first) suspended by a single rope from one of the higher cross members. More elaborate swings can be created from two lengths of rope and a single softwood plank. Alternatively, you can install a climbing rope—a single length of thick hemp rope with knots tied in it at regular intervals.

When making a swing use weather- and rot-proof nylon rope—you can buy it very cheaply at a yacht chandler's or (in the form of a car tow-rope) from a motor accessory shop.

To make a swing seat use PAR softwood rather than ply as solid timber is stronger round the edges. Buy an offcut at least 25mm thick and 150mm × 400mm in size and drill a 10mm hole on the exact centre line of the plank and not less than 30mm from the end.

Feed one rope through each hole, tie in it as big and tight a knot as you can to prevent it slipping back out again (fig. 12), and seal the cut end of the (nylon) rope by melting it with a flame. Then hang the swing from one of the frame members by passing the other ends of the ropes through a couple of

9 *Fit the two end battens on opposite sides of the top end of the gang plank, again using screws in counterbored holes for safety*

11 *Round off the corners of the side rails so that they can't splinter or otherwise hurt the children when they are using it*

bolt holes 400mm apart. Tie good, tight knots at the top, too (fig. 13).

A platform can be fun as well as useful— it makes it easier for the child to get to the slide, for one thing. Use 19mm marine ply cut to 1200mm × 745mm; any other board will warp. Apply several coats of marine varnish or exterior-quality paint and take care to flood the grain round all four edges. Screw the platform across two of the horizontal frame members using 50mm No. 8 brass woodscrews, ensuring that the screw heads are countersunk and then filled (fig. 14).

Finishing touches

Many owners will prefer to leave the frame out in the garden all year, some for only the summer months. Whichever is the case, the unit will get very wet—especially if it stands on grass. The best way to ensure a long life is to treat it with at least two coats of a water-repellent preservative stain. These stains come in several shades, are non-toxic and are easy to maintain—you simply brush on extra coats as needed. If you don't mind touching up scuffs and chips, you could use yacht varnish or exterior-quality paint. In this case, preparation is vital. All components should be sanded smooth and knot holes or indentations filled with a plastic filler. Apply several coats of wood preservative, then cover this either with the varnish

---

★ WATCH POINT ★

Whatever treatment you choose, remember to flood the endgrain of the frame components with preservative. Where the unit sits on grass or wet soil you may also wish to lay strips of bituminous felt under the feet of the lower frames to prevent too much water being drawn into the timber.

---

or with a complete treatment of primer, undercoat and finish paint.

If your garden isn't big enough for the climbing frame, or if you don't want such a big structure on the lawn, you could erect the frame indoors in a suitable 'playroom', or even keep it in the corner of the children's bedroom.

If you're going to do this, however, think of the carpets: lay some offcuts of 19mm plywood or blockboard under the feet of the frame to prevent deep and permanent marks

12 *Fix the rope to the swing seat by passing it through a hole near the edge of the timber and tying a tight figure-of-eight knot*

13 *You can use a figure-of-eight knot or a bow-line to secure swings or climbing ropes to the cross bars of the climbing frame*

14 *Cut the platform to whichever size you or your child wants and fix it using countersunk woodscrews. Remember to fill the screw holes*

15 *If you are erecting the climbing frame outdoors, coat all the components with preservative. Don't use creosote*

from appearing. There is also the question of balance to be considered —any slight inaccuracies in the length of the various legs will be offset in the garden as the frame 'sinks' slightly into the grass; in the bedroom they may cause the frame to rock slightly, so pack the feet out a little to stabilize it.

Part of the beauty of this frame is that it can also be erected on the side of a hill, even one with a marked slope. The technique is to bed the feet of the various frame members into the soil so that they stand four-square, with each adjoining frame slightly higher or lower than its neighbour to match the slope. For safety's sake you should brace the frame using a couple of lengths of rope and stout timber tent pegs driven into the ground 'uphill' from the frame to prevent it toppling over.

C. *The gang plank is simpler and safer than a ladder. The laminate slide surface on the other side is strictly optional*

half-round moulding at 200mm centres

plywood

laminate

battens 50mm × 50mm

edge strips 25mm × 12mm

MAKE A CHILD'S SANDPIT

Sandpits are always a great attraction and when combined with a paddling pool are guaranteed to provide hours of fun. With this design you can make both from the one basic plan.

Sandpits don't have to be very big, which means you should be able to fit one into even the smallest garden. Nor do they have to be expensive and complicated to construct. This design (fig. A) shows just what can be done with basic materials readily available from your local timber yard and hardware store. It also has the advantage that it can be modified to make a toddlers' paddling pool.

You could build both and set them together so your children can have a complete summer play area where you can keep an eye on them and yet there's plenty for them to do.

near to the house and clearly visible from the downstairs windows.

You'll need a flat site as the box rests directly on the ground. A large patio is ideal as it's easy to sweep away any sand that's scattered over the edge of the box. In this instance, saw off the 'drive in' fixing legs shown in the design and use angle brackets to secure the pit. Or you can simply rest it in place if you want to move it around quickly and easily.

A lawn provides another good site but you must bear in mind any adverse effects on the grass.

Try to set the box in a sunny position and keep it away from trees and bushes, which tend to attract insects. And falling leaves are nothing but an aggravating nuisance in damp sand.

What you need

Building the sandpit requires very few tools so a simple kit including a panel saw, screwdriver, drill and bits, and a mallet will suffice. If you are preparing a site in the garden you should also have a spade and rake. Some string and pegs will be useful in marking out the site.

The materials you need for the sandpit are a sheet of oil-tempered hardboard, and some exterior plywood for the top and bottom. The sides are cut from 230mm × 25mm softwood, the legs from 50mm × 50mm softwood, and the seats are cut from 150mm × 25mm softwood. For the framing of the top you'll need 50mm × 25mm softwood.

★ WATCH POINT ★

Make sure the lid is always put on after the children have finished playing in the pit or pool. This is important if for no other reason than keeping animals from fouling the play area. The lid will also prevent the sand being drenched in a downpour of rain. For reasons of hygiene it's probably best to empty the pool after it's been used but the lid will stop debris falling into it. Sandpits and paddling pools not used properly or without some form of supervision can give rise to accidents.

Siting the sandpit

Where you site the sandpit will very much depend on the size and shape of your garden. Remember that the pit isn't a permanent fixture and will only be used in the summer months. You could, if you wanted to, take it up and store it safely away in a shed or garage during the long winter months.

The most important consideration is one of **safety**, particularly in the case of paddling pools. Keep the sandpit or pool

Right: *This versatile sandpit, which can also be made into a paddling pool, will keep children amused for hours*

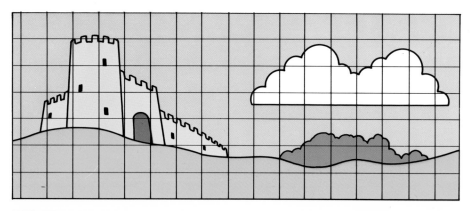

Alternatively, before you finish off with varnish, you can paint the sides of the boxes with a colourful design (fig. A). In this design, two have been included but you can use just about any source for your design.

To use this design, draw a similar grid on a piece of paper with 30mm squares. Use this as your guide to scale up the drawings. Then transfer the design to the side of the sandpit or pool. If you want to repeat the design several times cut a stencil. Once the paint has dried, completely seal the whole thing with several coats of varnish.

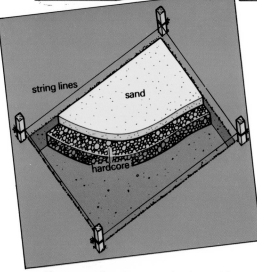

A. *Use the grid as a guide for transferring the design to the sides of the boxes. The castle in the desert is perfect for the sandpit, the tropical island ideal for the pool*

B. *Use string lines to mark out the sandpit and lay hardcore and sand*

important stages. Skimp on this and the pit or pool will not last for more than one summer. Both a sandpit and paddling pool are going to take a fair bashing from children and adverse weather conditions. So before you start any assembly work treat all the timber with a couple of coats of wood preservative. And if you want to change the colour of the wood, try one of the heavily pigmented types. Then later, when the boxes have been made up (and in the case of the pool, before the polyethylene liner has been added) and when all screw and nail heads have been covered up, coat everything with several coats of exterior-grade polyurethane varnish or gloss paint. This will give a tough surface resistant to water. It will also prevent splinters forming on which children could injure themselves while they're playing.

If you are planning to make the paddling pool as well, you will need some heavy-duty polyethylene for the liner and a sheet of vinyl flooring to lay on the base. You need glue and screws to assemble it all and to finish off, some exterior-grade polyurethane varnish or paint. Treat all of the softwood with a preservative after you've cut it but before assembly. Remember, the structure will be outside so even if you haven't made the pool the wood will need protection from the rain.

Finishing treatments

The finishing off work is one of the most

Preparing the site

Lawns and patios will provide you with a ready-made flat site. But if you want to

create a permanent site by itself, from an old vegetable plot or flower bed for example, you'll need to do some thorough preparatory work before you set the sandpit in the chosen place.

First, dig over the site, rake it out and tamp it down firmly. Then check for level in several directions using a spirit level set on a long straightedge. Adjust the ground accordingly. Mark out the position of the sandpit using stringlines or the base of the box itself. Decide on the material you want to use round the box and prepare the area surrounding the box position. Then lay the turf or paving material on the prepared surface.

Next, dig out the site of the box to 100mm–150mm below the surface, fill with hardcore and finish off with a binding layer of sand to allow for adequate drainage beneath the box (fig. B). By providing a dry base you'll help to prolong the life of the sandpit.

Building the sandpit box

Fig. C shows exactly how the sandpit and pool are constructed. Study this first, so you're sure you know how it fits together.

Start by cutting the oil-tempered hardboard base to size. As you'll probably have to buy a 2440mm × 1220mm sheet, the offcut can be used later for the base of the pool.

The rectangle for the base of the sandpit should measure 1500mm × 1200mm. The sides are cut from 230mm × 25mm softwood, the longer ones being 1456mm in length, and the shorter ones being

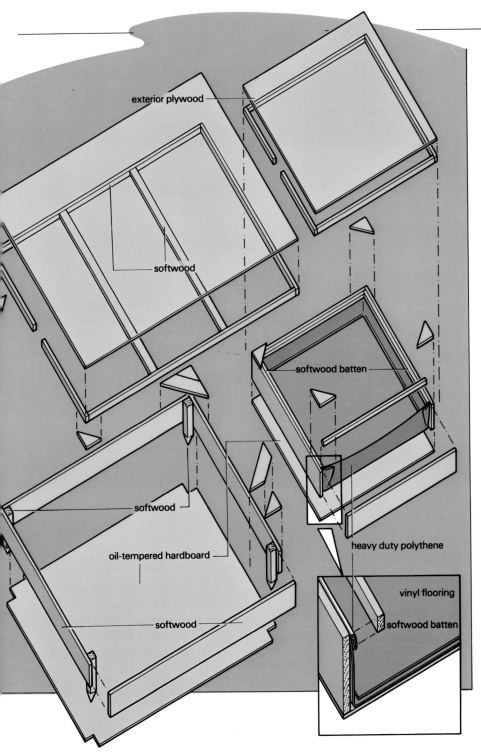

exterior plywood

softwood

softwood batten

softwood

oil-tempered hardboard

softwood

heavy duty polythene

vinyl flooring

softwood batten

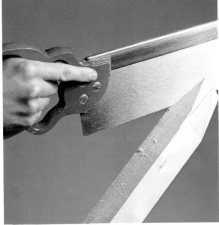

1 *Cut pointed ends on the legs—unless you plan to set the box on a paved area, in which case cut them to match the sides*

2 *Mark the screw positions on the legs and longer sides and drill pilot holes. Fix them together after countersinking the screw heads*

3 *Fix the shorter sides to the legs using the base as your guide. If the legs have been cut off they simply act as a corner brace*

1200mm in length. The four fixing legs should be 420mm long cut from 50mm × 50mm softwood. Cut pointed ends on the legs (fig. 1) so they can be driven into the ground. Remember, if you are setting the pit on a patio, cut the legs to the depth of the side of the box so that they simply become corner support battens.

Now glue and screw the legs to the inside faces of the longer side panels so that they are flush with their ends (fig. 2). Use a urea formaldehyde rather than a casein adhesive as the first will withstand all weather conditions. Drive four No. 8 50mm

C. *Both of the boxes are made from lengths of 230mm × 25mm softwood butt jointed at the corners. The legs are cut from 50mm × 50mm softwood cut to match the sides or with pointed ends. There are corner seats which act as bracing cut from 150mm × 25mm softwood, as well as similar spacing blocks for the lid. The base is cut from oil-tempered hardboard with notches cut out as necessary. The lids consist of exterior plywood set on a 50mm × 25mm batten frame. The pool is similar but has no legs. The liner is secured by a batten*

woodscrews through from the panel side to hold the legs in place. Space them evenly and countersink and fill over their heads.

When all the side panels are fixed together you'll have a free-standing unit. Now you have to fit the base. If you are building a box with legs, mark the position of the legs at the corners before taking the side panels off the hardboard (fig. 4). Remove the side panels and cut out the corners of the base along the lines. You will then be able to set the hardboard in position so that the legs pass through the notches cut in the base.

At this stage it's probably best to let the glue dry for a few hours and get on with the job of making the lid (see below). All that remains is to fit the base and the planks across two of the corners. Apart from acting as seats they also give extra rigidity to the top edges of the sandpit (fig. 5).

Hold each plank at an angle across the corners so that the ends of the leading edge rest on the edges of the side panels. Pencil along the underside of the plank where it

★ WATCH POINT ★

Lay the hardboard base on the ground with the shiny side up. Use this as a guide for squareness when you butt up the two shorter side panels and fix them to the other outward-facing edges of the legs (fig. 3). You'll find it easier if you work with the timber upside down so that the top edges of the box are set against the base held on the ground.

meets the side panels to give you the correct angle for cutting off the overlaps. Then glue and screw the seats in place.

Once the glue has dried turn the box upside down to fit the base to the frame (fig. 6). Glue and nail, with broad-headed annular copper-coated nails, to hold the board in place. The shiny side should be the side that eventually comes into contact with the ground. If there are no fixing legs,

simply nail the base straight to the bottom of the side panels.

Now set the box in place in the garden. If it has fixing legs, these will have to be driven in with a mallet. Work so that the box settles down on to the ground evenly so as little strain as possible is put on the joints. Half fill the box with silver sand once it is securely in position.

Making the lid

The lid is made of 6mm thick exterior-grade plywood attached to a 50mm × 50mm softwood batten frame. The lengths of the framing members correspond to the dimensions of the box itself. Cut the top of the lid to match the base.

Make up the frame first on top of the plywood as you did the box, butt jointing and nailing the sections together (fig. 7). This will ensure that the frame and plywood fit flush around the edges. Drive the nails below the surface and fill the holes. Transfer

4 *With care, turn the box upside down and mark the lines for cutting the notches in the hardboard to fit round the supporting legs*

5 *Glue and screw the corner seats in place to help keep the box square. Use two pieces set side by side for each seat*

6 *Turn the box over and fit the hardboard base to the frame with copper-coated nails, keeping the shiny side facing out*

10 *Assemble the basic box by gluing and pinning the butt joints together. Then fit the base as you did for the sandpit*

11 *Cut an oversize square of heavy duty polyethylene and lay it over the box. Then work it well down into the corners*

12 *Lay the square of flooring vinyl so that it sits evenly on the base of the box and holds the polyethylene in place*

the position of the frame to the top surface of the plywood then glue and screw the frame and sheet together (fig. 8).

Because the lid rests on top of the two corner seats, it stands to reason that if left like this it wouldn't sit level on top of the sandpit. Glue and screw small angle braces to the underside of the lid framework to match the two corners of the sandpit which are not fitted with seats (fig. 9).

Leave a 150mm gap in the framework along one side to make it easy to grip the lid to lift it off the box.

Making the paddling pool

The basic principles of the sandpit can be easily adapted to make a small paddling pool. The base of the paddling pool is made of oil-tempered hardboard cut to 900mm square. Cut two sides from 230mm × 25mm softwood 900mm long as well as two shorter sides 856mm long. These are butted together, glued and pinned securely (fig. 10). Because of the size of the pool, internal corner supports are unnecessary. In fact their presence would make it awkward to fit the pool liner. Extra rigidity is given to the framework later by screwing triangular corner seats to the top edge. The pool won't need fixing legs as you'll need to be able to tip it up to run out the water after each use.

Once the frame has been assembled, lay the heavy-duty polyethylene over it, tucking the sheet well down into the bottom corners of the box (fig. 11). Then set the square of heavy-duty vinyl over the base (an offcut will do)—this will help to keep the polyethylene in place (fig. 12). It will also provide a more comfortable surface for your children to stand on. And it can be removed easily for cleaning.

You may find it a little difficult to get the polyethylene to form neat corners. The best method is to pleat it and then use PVC adhesive to hold the various folds in place (fig. 13). Don't be tempted to pin it to the side walls, as this will only cause the paddling pool to leak noticeably when it is full of water.

Finally, you've got to fix the polyethylene to the top of the box above the water line. You could just lap it over the top edge and pin it, but then there's the possibility of the children cutting their feet on the exposed nail heads. Instead, fold the sheeting down until it is just below the top. Screw battens against it to pinch it in position, and countersink the screw heads (fig. 14). It doesn't matter about piercing the sheeting at this level because this will be above the water line when the pool is filled. Now screw on all the corner seats which help give the box its necessary rigidity of structure (fig. 15).

The lid is constructed in exactly the same way as for the sand pit, but, because it is smaller, it will need only perimeter battening: cross battening is unnecessary. Nor will it need extra supporting blocks in the corners as there are already four seats giving the lid a level bedding on which it can firmly rest.

7 *Assemble the framework for the lid on top of the plywood using it as your guide to ensure that the frame is square*

8 *Nail the top of the lid to the framework and drive the heads below the surface. Fill the holes and sand the filler when hard*

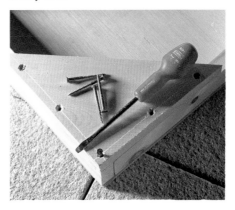

9 *Fix braces to the lid at the corners opposite the seat positions so that the lid sits evenly all round when it is set in place*

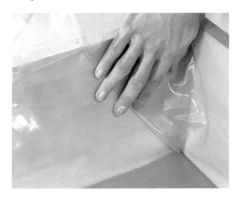

13 *Carefully pleat all the corners of the polyethylene liner and use blobs of PVC adhesive to hold it securely in place*

14 *Trim the edges of the polyethylene with a sharp knife and roll it over. Clamp it to the box by fitting a batten with screws*

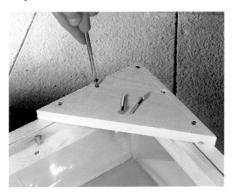

15 *Finally add the four corner angle pieces which act as small seats and also give the necessary bracing support to the framework*

CHAPTER 6

OUTBUILDINGS

The budding gardener needs a store for the selection of tools and equipment vital to horticultural activities and there's few structures to beat the ubiquitous timber shed. It's attractive and useful in any garden and the ideal protection for a host of items: proprietary kits make self-assembly so easy. If you want to extend your growing season, or to concentrate on raising more exotic blooms, you'll need a greenhouse. But you don't have to resort to buying the frequently expensive modern metal types; building your own design from timber isn't complicated if you follow these basic instructions.

BUILD A GARDEN SHED

If you lack storage space for your garden tools, a timber shed could solve all your problems. They're available in a range of sizes to suit all gardens and are no problem to build providing you follow one or two basic rules.

A garden shed is always useful as a place to lock away your garden tools and equipment, bikes and deckchairs, as well as a place to pot plants and store them over winter. A larger shed with good window light and good headroom can even be used as a small workshop.

Most garden buildings are wooden, but you can also get metal sheds and sheds with concrete-panel walls. Metal sheds will last a lifetime, but they are utilitarian and, unlike the more natural-looking timber shed, are out of place in most gardens. Concrete-panel sheds are really an alternative to building in brick and are considerably more expensive than a wooden building.

Choosing a size

The most popular size for a shed is just over two metres deep by about one and a half metres wide. This gives plenty of storage space and room for a narrow waist-height shelf or a fold-away workbench. If you want a shed just for storage, or if space is very tight, you might consider a much smaller shed of about one metre square with double doors. Although not large enough to step into, the advantage of such a shallow shed is that storage is easy to organize and there are no dark depths for things to get lost in.

A shed of about three metres by two and a half metres with plenty of window light (and perhaps an electricity supply) will give you enough room for a permanent workbench.

The size of shed you choose may be influenced by where you intend to site it— think carefully about this. Sheds are often put at the far end of a garden where they are out of sight; but it may be more convenient to have a shed much nearer the house where there is a dry mud-free path and it is fairly easy and not too expensive to fix up an electricity supply.

Choose a site which is level and avoid parts of the garden that tend to be wet or boggy. Position the shed out of the main lines of view from the house; if it has to be built in sight, arrange rambling plants such as evergreen clematis or honeysuckle, to

Above: *Garden sheds are now readily available in kit form. They are easy to build and different sizes can be obtained to suit your garden*

soften the harsh lines of the design.

If you want to use your shed as a growing house, make sure the windows get good sunlight, otherwise put your shed in shade so that the more sunny parts of the garden can be used for flowerbeds. Think about the way the door will open and aim to have the opening away from the prevailing wind.

Buying a shed

Before committing yourself to buying a particular shed, have a look at a sample that has been erected (even mail-order firms have showrooms where their sheds are available for inspection). Look for a shed

that has all the features you want and then check that the structure is sound. Fig. A shows three popular types.

Take particular note of the following points:
- **Roof:** There are two types of roof: apex—with sloping sides either side of a ridge; and pent—with a slope in only one direction. Pent roofs are used on shallow sheds and on low-priced ones of average size—they look best when a shed is installed with a wall or fence behind; a shed with an apex roof looks good whether free-standing or alongside a wall.
- **Cladding:** The wooden cladding of the shed walls can be simple overlap, rebated or tongued-and-grooved. Overlapping cladding is most economical and used on cheaper sheds; rebating gives better water-proofing and, provided good quality timber is used, tongued-and-grooved is more weatherproof still. You may come across

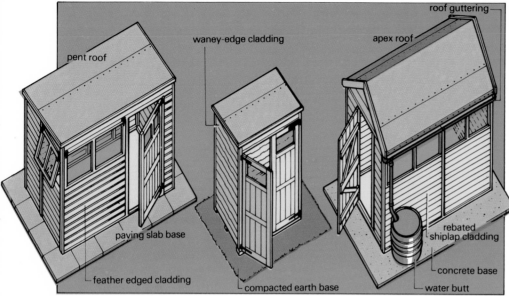

labels: pent roof, waney-edge cladding, roof guttering, apex roof, paving slab base, feather edged cladding, compacted earth base, shiplap cladding, rebated shiplap cladding, concrete base, water butt

A. *Three types of garden shed and how they are constructed. The more elaborate the construction, the more expensive the shed, and therefore the more durable it will be*

another shed. Check fixings as well: are nails straight, holes properly drilled and so on?

In your shed kit you should get:
- **prefabricated panels:** sides, ends, roof slopes, floor (if required) and door;
- **window frames** (these may be glazed);
- **ironmongery:** nuts, bolts and hinges;
- **door lock:** with the better kits;
- **instructions** for assembly.

You may also need:
- **preservative** if the shed is not pretreated —buy either a proprietary timber preservative or traditional creosote;
- **rag bolts or expanding anchor bolts** to secure the shed to the base;
- **concrete** for a solid floor—mix cement: damp sand:coarse aggregate in the ratio $1:1\frac{2}{3}:2\frac{2}{3}$;
- **lock** for door if not supplied;
- **cup hooks** and shelf brackets;

shiplap cladding, this can be rebated or tongued-and-grooved—the name describes the shape of the board.
- **Floor:** A boarded floor on framing bearers is available as an optional extra with most sheds. These are useful if you are installing the shed on sleeper walls or if you want a floor which is 'warm' underfoot. A shed on a concrete slab base can be constructed without a boarded floor.
- **Timber:** Sheds are available in redwood, whitewood and Western Red Cedar. The first two are softwoods, which need treating with preservative for durability. Some sheds are sold untreated for you to do yourself, but a shed will last longer if it's professionally treated and it is worth paying the extra for a shed that has been pressure-impregnated with a preservative.

Western Red Cedar is naturally durable. Left untreated it weathers to an attractive grey; if you prefer the timber to be light brown you will need to revive the surface with an occasional brushed-on cedar treatment.
- **Doors and windows:** Apex roof sheds usually have the door at the centre on one end. Pent roof sheds may have the door on an end or on the front. A front-opening door is ideal for a shed to be used only for storage, but if you want a workbench or a shelf for plants, an end door is better as it leaves the long side uninterrupted. Doors are normally single ledged-and-braced, but sometimes part glazed durable doors are offered. The windows are normally along one side.

If you want to use your shed partly as a growing house look for a shed with windows at 45° above a cantilevered shelf to give even light to plants. If you want

opening windows for ventilation, look for top-hinged ones which can be left open in the rain.

To check the structure of the shed, shake the walls, slam the door, and jump on the floor—if it bends or feels fragile look for

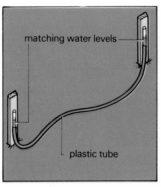

labels: matching water levels, plastic tube

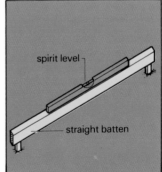

labels: spirit level, straight batten

B. *(far left) When preparing a shed site, if the stakes are far apart, use a clear, water-filled tube to check the level. When water levels match, the ground is even*

C. *(left) When stakes are close together use a spirit level*

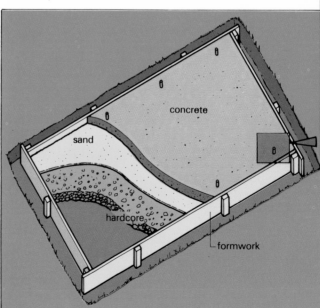

labels: concrete, sand, hardcore, formwork

label: rag bolt

D. *A concrete raft is the most stable foundation for a shed, but can be expensive. The hardcore must be about 75mm deep, the sand 25mm, and the concrete 75mm. Bed rag bolts (inset) in wet concrete to secure walls*

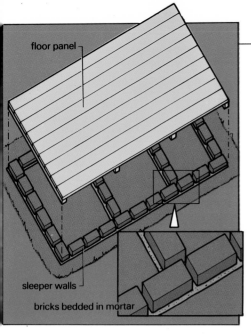

floor panel

sleeper walls

bricks bedded in mortar

E. *Sleeper walls, a single layer of bricks high and embedded on mortar, will support most sheds easily. Leave gaps between bricks to allow air to circulate freely and prevent dampness which would almost certainly lead to rot in the floor—this should be laid on bitumen damp proofing felt*

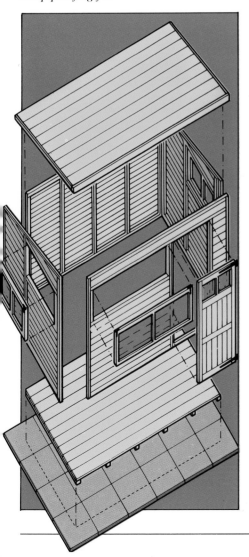

F. *The major components of a typical garden shed kit with a pent roof. Apex roof models are only slightly more complicated. The base is of level paving slabs butted tight together; these should overlap the shed base. Construction is simple, all the components being nailed or screwed together*

● **bitumen damp-proof course:** available in roll form.

Tools

Make sure that you have all your tools to hand before you start work. You will need:
● **a spanner** of appropriate size;
● **hammer** and pins for glazing;
● **trowel,** spade, wheelbarrow (for concrete);
● **side forms** and stepladder;
● **brace and bit** or electric drill and bit (if holes aren't predrilled) and a putty knife.

Preparing the site

It's important to choose the correct site for your shed. One of the main requirements is that it should be level.

One of the best ways of checking levels is to use a water level (fig. B)—a length of polyethylene tube like that supplied for home brewing, full of water with a cork in each end. You can use this to set stakes to exactly the same level—the stake tops are level when the water level at each end of the tube coincides with each mark.

For a small job like a shed base it may be just as easy to set pairs of stakes level by laying a batten and spirit level across the pair (fig. C)—but beware of cumulative errors with this method.

Stakes can easily be prepared by sawing at a steep angle through a length of rough sawn batten. Wooden tent pegs are an alternative. Use nylon string rather than hemp, as this may well rot or stretch if it is left in the open.

Laying the floor

Laying the floor is the first job to be done, and the one which makes most difference to the finish of your shed. Mark out roughly the site for your shed and set string guidelines around the area to be cleared. Clear any vegetation and remove the fertile topsoil for use elsewhere in the garden. If the area is grassed, lift the turfs in pieces

300mm × 100mm, roll them up and keep to use elsewhere.

For a solid base establish the exact size that the base needs to be and move your stringlines to suit these critical dimensions. At this stage it is important to work precisely—if the base ends up too large it will collect water and the puddles will rot the lower timbers of the shed. The slab is usually made 38mm smaller than the shed itself. Take care to get the corners at 90°.

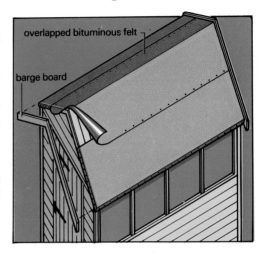

overlapped bituminous felt

barge board

G. *On an apex roof lay roofing felt starting from the 'bottom' of the roof, with a single piece covering the ridge, then add fascias*

On some soils it is possible to lay a concrete slab directly on the subsoil, but an unstable soil, such as shrinkable clay or peat, needs a 75mm layer of hardcore beneath the concrete (fig. D).

Find a source of clean hardcore such as builders' rubble from which the perishable bits such as paper and wood have been sorted. Before laying the hardcore, dose the soil liberally with weedkiller to prevent plant growth breaking up the foundations.

★ WATCH POINT ★

To check that your rectangle is exactly true measure the diagonals—these should be equal.

Break up the hardcore with a sledge-hammer into pieces small enough to mingle without voids, then compact it well.

Level the hardcore surface with a layer of sand (a 50kg bag will cover 3 sq metres) or, if you are not laying hardcore, lay the sand on the subsoil about 25mm deep. Place a sheet of 250 gauge polyethylene over the

★ WATCH POINT ★

Formwork is normally made from lengths of timber, but it may be cheaper to hire steel road forms for this purpose. A weekend's hire should suffice.

sand to extend beyond the stringlines and weight it temporarily with bricks. Fix a formwork box over the polyethylene to hold a depth of 75mm concrete in the area bounded by the strings.

Arrange planks on to and across the formwork as access for a wheelbarrow so that you can pour the concrete evenly in the area to be filled. Use a stout timber to ram the mix well into the corners and for firm edges work along the formwork. Use a plank on edge to 'saw' the concrete level with the formwork, top up any hollows and saw again.

While the concrete is still wet, work out where the base will sit and position rag bolts to secure the edges of the shed—two or three on each side is usually enough.

You can leave the concrete with its sawn finish or, for a floor that can be swept more easily, smooth the surface lightly with a trowel about an hour after the concrete has been placed.

★ WATCH POINT ★

If you have to lay concrete in hot weather, cover it with something to retain the moisture—and spray it if it shows signs of drying out. If frost threatens, cover the concrete with newspaper held in place by a poly-ethylene sheet.

Board flooring

A board floor can be laid directly on a firm subsoil, but it is much better to provide a solid base—a concrete slab as above or sleeper walls around the perimeter and under the main bearers (fig. E). The walls need only be one brick (or block) high. Often you can lay them straight on com-pacted earth, but the base is more secure if you bed the bricks on mortar—the mortar is also useful to take up any unevenness in levels. It is essential that the sleeper walls are level to provide equal and even support

1 *Whichever type of base you finally select, lay a damp proof course over it before laying the floor panels and their timber bearers*

5 *Use coach bolts to secure the walls firmly to each other, tightening the nuts from inside where they won't be affected by rust*

9 *Offer up the roof panels, nailing them to the roof supports once you are satisfied they butt together and cover the entire shed*

2 *Skew-nail through one floor panel into the timber bearer supporting the adjacent one, then nail the adjacent battens together*

6 *Fit the windows then the roof supports, screwing them in place from inside the shed where water cannot drip into the holes*

10 *Overlap the bituminous felt generously, with the overlap running 'downhill' to allow rain to run off without soaking the timber*

3 *While an assistant holds the wall panels up from the 'outside', nail them temporarily together inside, ensuring they are square*

4 *When the walls are square, nail them to the floor while your assistant supports them from outside in the vertical plane*

7 *Apex roofs must be tough, especially on a large shed. Extra bracing is necessary to prevent sagging and leaks*

8 *Don't rely on nails and screws to carry much weight. Ensure that roofs and rafters are supported by the vertical frame members*

11 *Lay the bituminous felt roof covering on the roof panels and nail the fascia board in place on the higher edge of the roof*

12 *To protect tools and garden furniture (and to satisfy your insurance company) fit proper door and window locks before you store things*

to the floor. Lay the bricks with larger joints than for normal bricklaying and leave the spaces between them clear of mortar so air can circulate underneath.

A popular alternative to concrete slabs and sleeper floors is a layer of concrete paving slabs. These come in a variety of sizes and colours so choose the type you prefer and buy enough to overlap the shed base all round.

Clear the site, remove the turf if you wish, and level and compact the earth. Apply a liberal dose of weedkiller to prevent vegetation growing up between the slabs. Mark the exact size of the base with stakes and string, and lay the slabs one by one, using the stringlines and a spirit level to ensure they are all horizontal and on the same plane. Fill hollows with fine hardcore or gravel.

Use a couple of extra slabs as a 'doorstep' to prevent the grass being worn away outside the shed door and to prevent puddles forming after rain.

Before installing the floor on a concrete slab, paving slabs or sleeper walls, lay strips of bitumen damp-proof course under the bearers to halt rising damp.

Assembling the kit

By making sure that you have all the parts of your kit ready (fig. F) before you start and sorting out the fixing you will need at each stage, you'll find assembling the shed is quite a simple process.

First of all, lay the floor on the base (fig. 1). With a boarded floor screw down to the framing bearers (joists) underneath the boards; with a concrete floor you will need to use masonry anchor bolts if you haven't already set rag bolts in the concrete. Nail the floor panels on to the timber bearers (fig. 2).

Unless you're prepared to mess around with temporary braces, you will need a helper to hold the wall panels while you fix them together. In some sheds the panels are simply bolted together through predrilled holes, but it is only a little more time consuming to use screws in pilot holes you make yourself with a hand drill or a brace and bit. There are normally three fixing points at each corner of the shed. The panels are arranged so that the bottom batten slightly overlaps the edge of the floor (or concrete base). When all four side panels are in place fix the panels to the floor.

With the frame secure, you can fit the windows (fig. 6), the roof bearers (figs 7 and 8) followed by the roof panels (fig. 9). They may be notched to fit over the wall panels. Fixing is either by metal angle brackets or by screwing through the purlins and top battens of the panels. Access to brackets is normally a little easier.

With some sheds the roof panels are supplied prefelted so all that remains at this stage is to tighten the panel fixings and then finish off. If the roof is not prefelted, fix the felt supplied. It will normally be a one metre wide lightweight bitumen felt surfaced with tiny mineral granules.

★ WATCH POINT ★

It will be easier to fix the felt (and you'll avoid problems with stretching) if you lay it unrolled in a warm place for a day before fitting.

Lay the felt horizontally, starting from the lower edge. Allow an overlap of at least 25mm on all nail edges (fig. 10) and nail the felt to the roof panel framing timbers at 100mm intervals. Use 19mm galvanized large-headed clout nails if nails are not supplied. Do this on both sides of an apex roof and then lay the crown felt to go over the ridge board and down each side to overlap the lower felts by at least 75mm (fig. G). Some kits include bitumen adhesive to seal this joint, but it isn't strictly necessary; nailing through both layers of felt into a roof purlin is usually adequate.

In areas where torrential rain and heavy winds are common it is a good idea to seal the overlap between layers of roofing felt. Lay a course of mastic between the two layers along the line where you will nail the upper one to the roof panel.

Finish the roof by nailing on the fascia boards (fig. 11) and any capping supplied. Fit the felt over battens if any are supplied. All these timbers are very exposed, so give them an extra preservative treatment (by soaking if possible) to ensure durability.

Finishing the shed

The quality of finishing greatly enhances the durability and character of the shed so don't cut any corners. Hang the shed door using the hinges supplied—usually black japanned tee hinges (they should be about a third of the door long). The holes for the hinge screws may be predrilled; if not you will need to do this job yourself. Get someone to hold the door while you mark the positions. Remember to allow a clearance of

13 *Secure the glass (or clear acrylic sheet) with putty on one side and sprigs or headless pins on the other, forcing the sheet against the putty*

15 *Although the timber should be pre-treated it is wise to add a further coat of preservative—it's available in a variety of colours*

6mm at the bottom.

If you bolt the hinges on (with the nuts on the inside) it makes it difficult for anyone to remove the door from outside. The same applies to a hasp and staple fixing for a padlock. This is the minimum security you will need for a shed, although a sturdy door lock is better (fig. 12). Note that household insurance policies often exclude garden equipment stolen from unlocked outbuildings.

Windows will usually need glazing, although most shed suppliers provide the glass. If you break a piece, replace it with horticultural glass—optically this is not as good as the float glass used for house windows but it is cheaper.

Putty may be supplied for bedding the glass at the back only, with special sprigs to hold it in place (fig. 13). If putty is sticky rub it on a clear sheet of paper to remove excess oil.

Nail vertical battens to both sides of the corners to protect the vulnerable end grain

14 *Fit vertical battens at the corners to protect the end grain of the cladding panels from the weather, and as an extra brace*

of the cladding panels (fig. 14).

If your shed was not pre-treated with preservative use an old brush and apply creosote or preservative liberally (fig. 15); work from the bottom of the shed up to the roof so that splashes won't stain untreated parts. Take care not to splash plants or get the chemicals on your skin. Creosote is poisonous to plants, but preservatives are usually not.

Shelves and hooks are the finishing touches inside. Make sure any shelf bracket is properly supported by a strong framing member of the shed. Use spring clips to provide tidy storage for long-handled equipment such as rakes and brooms and store them head up with any teeth facing the wall.

Timber sheds—especially old, dry, weathered ones—burn easily. If you install an electricity supply, ensure that this is properly earthed and that the components are regularly maintained and not overloaded: sparks and overheating can char the timber and cause fires. Electricity should only be installed by a competent person. If you're not exactly sure what to do, seek expert advice.

When storing plants over the winter, take care over the use of paraffin heaters. These are normally quite safe, but make sure they cannot tip over accidentally and start a fire.

If using the shed as a work room, you will inevitably need some sort of heating during the winter months. Portable gas heaters are perfectly safe if used properly: ensure there is adequate ventilation and that the burners operate correctly—carbon monoxide kills. Also make sure that the gas bottle is disconnected when not in use. Gas leaks can cause an explosion.

Finally, if storing lawnmower fuel or weedkiller, *label the containers clearly*.

BUILDING A GREENHOUSE

In temperate climates, the growing season for many plants in the open is short, and this is bound to restrict your choice of plants and flowers. But a greenhouse can alter the situation completely, enabling plants of many kinds to be grown all the year round. In colder climates, an even greater variety of plants can be propagated and grown if the greenhouse is continually heated, as this will allow you to grow many different exotic examples from warmer regions all around the world.

Building your own greenhouse is not a very complicated job, and it permits you to design and tailor the building to suit your individual needs, the requirements of the site, and the type of plants that you wish to grow.

This section gives you information on the different types of greenhouse you can construct and the step-by-step pictures show you how to build the easy lean-to style of greenhouse which is pictured on this page.

Basic considerations

One of the first things to decide is the type of crop to be grown, noting any special requirements; for example, indoor carnations grow best in tall greenhouses, and need more ventilation than most crops. If you are uncertain about the most suitable greenhouse for your needs consult a nursery or an experienced gardener. However, for average purposes, it is usually a matter of selecting a convenient and sunny spot, either making use of an existing wall to build a lean-to greenhouse, or alternatively siting it apart from other buildings as a free-standing unit.

The size and type of greenhouse best

A. Below: *A lean-to greenhouse is a pot planter's paradise and an asset to any home. In it you can be 'outside' and relax even when the weather is bad—and it is far cheaper than an extension*

suited to your needs are partly governed by the space available, the site itself, the crops and the final cost.

The lean-to type, best sited on an east–west axis in the sun, is usually cheaper to make, to heat (because of its better insulation), and to maintain than a free-standing model of similar size and construction. The mini greenhouse variation can be either a lean-to or free-standing type (see below).

Available space may be further restricted by planning regulations. Structures in front of the building line between the house and the road are normally prohibited in the UK. On the other hand, small greenhouses which are less than 3m high and which do not occupy more than half the garden area are not usually subject to planning consent. Unless you are absolutely certain of the planning regulations in your area, you should consult the local council before starting work.

Design and construction

All buildings have a number of important design and construction requirements, and in the case of a greenhouse there are six main considerations.
- **Appearance:** This is influenced by the design and also by the construction materials—usually wood and glass.
- **Strength and durability:** A greenhouse should be capable of withstanding the worst possible conditions of wind, sun, storms, frost and snow. Timber glazing bars, for example, should ideally not be less than 20mm deep for a 1m span, and the depth should be increased by 12mm for each additional 500mm of span.
- **Light:** Maximum light is of course necessary all the year round so avoid narrowly spaced glazing bars, aiming for intervals of between 450mm and 750mm.
- **Ventilation:** This is critical; the total ventilator area should ideally not be less than 15 per cent or one-sixth of the floor space.
- **Ease of construction:** It is very important that a greenhouse project does not demand great expense on tools and materials, and in this respect a timber frame is a good choice.
- **Low maintenance:** Costs need to be kept in mind, and simplicity of design, combined with sound construction techniques, are of great importance.

Comparison with kits

When deciding whether to erect a proprietary kit greenhouse, or to build a home-made unit, the acid test for most people boils down to cost; but to make a valid comparison you have to take into account many factors, including quality, design, construction and durability. Often the kit price excludes such items as the base, the glass and delivery, so the comparison must be made on the cost of the different greenhouses erected on site complete. This way you can make a fair assessment of relative costs.

Different models

Although the following describes how to build two lean-to types of greenhouse, a free-standing span or apex type with a high central ridge or a mini greenhouse can also be made with certain modifications.

Timber is excellent for the main structure because it is versatile and easy to work with, and presents few problems with either glazing or cladding. Also, less condensation forms on wooden frames than on metal ones because they retain a more even temperature. Given the occasional treatment with paint or preservative, timber structures can last 20 to 30 years and more.

Softwood should be treated with a horticultural grade of preservative containing copper naphthanate. Special attention should be paid to joints and those parts of the building which are in contact with the ground. These should be soaked for a few days in a container of the solution. Long timbers such as bottom plates can be laid on a long sheet of polyethylene gathered along the corners and edges to form a receptacle or bag into which preservative is poured.

Although it costs about 50 per cent more, cedar wood is a timber which requires little treatment or maintenance because it has a natural oil which resists

1 *First prepare the site, providing an even bed of hardcore which should be well tamped down, and paint the back wall with a weatherproof agent*

2 *Having cut the back horizontal and vertical timbers and applied a timber preservative, fix the horizontal wall plate with long coach bolts*

6 *The bottom plate of the front frame is a structural component and so it should be firmly fixed to the building blocks with wall anchors*

7 *At this stage apply a liberal amount of timber preservative to the bottom plate, making quite certain that you treat all cuts and end grain*

decay and is ideal for outdoor use.

Both the lean-to greenhouse designs are made up of four sections—two ends, the front and the roof. The designs as shown are adequate for a greenhouse with an eaves height of 1.52m, a ridge height of 2.13m and a width of 2.33m. This should allow considerable freedom of movement, but the measurements can easily be adapted to your own requirements, especially the length. However, if and when altering sizes, keep in mind the standard sizes of cladding materials: this avoids needless cutting and subsequent waste. Also, when building larger structures, heavier timbers and bracing are necessary for extra strength.

The four frames of the greenhouse can be assembled in one or two ways. The frames can be made up separately, then bolted together and screwed to the wall. Alternatively, the wall timbers or studs can be

screwed to the wall first, and the framework then constructed in situ. The frame can later be glazed or clad with PVC corrugated roofing sheet. Standard 4mm thick glass is adequate for glazing and this should be installed in 'modules' as nearly square as possible. This means in effect that the glass is panelled. For instance, on the roof, each run of glass between timbers consists of three panes of overlapping glass. This avoids the use of large panes of glass which are both vulnerable and difficult to install.

3 *Once the loadbearing wall plate has been fixed the vertical back frame can be secured to the wall using masonry nails*

4 *Lay a single course of lightweight building blocks then mortar treated posts into the hollow corner blocks. Make sure that the posts are vertical*

5 *In order to save much wasteful trimming of the cladding material, it makes sense to use it as a guide when actually building the structure*

8 *Once the preservative is dry, set the bottom plate on the building blocks. Make sure that it is flat, then render the building block course*

9 *The PVC roofing sheets can be secured to the structure either with battens or in grooves—the latter being easy to make with a circular saw*

10 *The essence of the greenhouse structure is that the frame is self-bracing. The front top plate is thus nailed to the front corner posts*

Making the four frames is very simple. The essence of the separate parts is that they are self-bracing, in other words they have an intrinsic strength in their unassembled state. The following is only a guide, however, and you should feel free to modify the construction if you want to change the dimensions.

End frame: Using planed softwood timber, cut the base, top, back and front to size then make half-lap angle joints at the ends using a tenon saw and chisel. Make T-halving joints to take the upright and horizontal timbers; these in turn are then cut to size with half-lap joints at the ends. The joints in the top rail must, of course, be cut to the appropriate angle.

In all cases, paint the prepared cuts with preservative before putting them together. Drill and countersink two screw holes at each joint to take the appropriate screws.

Do, however, avoid drilling too deep or the screws will have an insufficient grip. Finally, assemble the timber sections and screw them together, making sure that the bottom corners are perfectly square.

End frame with door: Preparation and assembly of the parts is the same as for the first end frame, but with three differences. The lower horizontal timber cross rail from the front stops at the centre upright instead of running through to the back. This allows for the door. Also necessary is a projecting vertical door stop fixed behind the centre upright and aligned with the door.

The door itself is made from two uprights, fixed to three cross pieces with half-lap joints at the ends and T-halving joints in the centre. Drill and countersink the appropriate screws as before. Then fix three 150mm 'T' hinges to the cross members of the door. The door should not actually be

hung until the end frames are fastened to the wall, but check that the door fits the frame before erecting the structure and adjust as necessary.

Front frame: Cut the four upright timbers to the correct length, making T-halving joints in the centres. Then cut the top, centre and base members, with half-lap end joints, plus two evenly spaced T-halving joints on each. Paint all joints with preservative and allow this to dry before drilling and countersinking to take two screws at each joint. Finally, assemble and screw the timbers together, making sure that the corners are square and that the bottom plate is laid flat side down like those of the end frames. If you decide to put a door in the front frame, follow the instructions given above. As before, do not hang the door until the structure is complete, but do make sure that it fits the frame before moving on to assemble the greenhouse.

Roof: Repeat as for the front frame, with the addition of a ventilator seating. Cut the ventilator seating timber with half-lap joints at each end and screw this securely into the extended half-lap joints of the two centre timbers. Because of the sloping roof it is necessary to chamfer the back timber by about 7°, just sufficiently to allow it to butt squarely against the wall when fixed to the wall plate. Make the ventilator frame in the same way as the door, with the necessary size adjustments. Fix two 150mm strap hinges to the roof frame for the ventilating system and make sure that it is a good weatherproof fit.

Foundations

The base of the greenhouse must be raised above the ground level, to keep it clear of surface water.

If you are building on soil then you will have to dig a foundation to provide a base, the top of which should be at least 25mm above ground level (fig. 1).

It may be that there will be an existing foundation of sorts, in the form of a drive-way, path or patio. Provided this consists of paving slabs or concrete laid over a hardcore base it will be adequate, although the level will still have to be raised to the proper height.

One way of doing this is to fit a formwork of 25mm × 25mm battening around the base and fill it with concrete. If you use this method, you must ensure that the new concrete bonds well to the existing surface by coating the latter with a solution of PVA bonding agent.

An alternative is to 'build' the base by laying paving slabs or a layer of bricks—with mortared joints in between them—on the top of the existing surface.

Whichever method you choose, the finished surface must be painted with a proprietary waterproof sealing compound.

A far simpler method of isolating the timber frame from the ground is to build a single course of lightweight building blocks

★ WATCH POINT ★

The base must be absolutely level when finished otherwise the wooden frames of the greenhouse will be at staggered heights when you come to assemble them and therefore they will not fit.

11 *Where thin section timbers are butt or halving jointed it is best to secure them with a screw. Always drill holes to avoid splitting the wood*

12 *Housing joints are normally skew-nailed, but a galvanized steel angle bracket screwed under the joint provides added strength*

14 *The PVC sheet can be cut using an abrasive disc fitted to a circular saw or saw attachment. Use a stout length of timber as a fence*

15 *When fixing the PVC cladding, support the sheets from below and from behind then drill through them and into the supporting timber*

17 *The window sill is fixed above the bottom cladding to provide a weather seal. All metal fittings must be of a type suitable for outdoor use*

18 *One great advantage of cladding the greenhouse with PVC roof sheeting is that it can be stretched or squashed up to take up minor adjustments*

13 *Alternatively, screw through joints after drilling and plugging the end grain of the longitudinal timber to avoid splitting it with the screw*

16 *Use pre-formed polystyrene eaves filler strips when fitting the roof to provide rigidity and also to draughtproof the greenhouse*

19 *With the end of the roof butted against the backing wall, the joint can be made weathertight with a timber batten, mastic and self-adhesive flashing*

on top of a shallow 150mm concrete foundation, then lay the bottom plates on the frames. Using this method, the two front corner posts, suitably preserved, may be anchored into hollow blocks, and the rest of the structure constructed about these (fig. 4). If the course is continued around the floor area, there will be a step at the base of the door. If you feel that this is a disadvantage, the blocks and bottom plate can be constructed with a cutout for the door. However, without the step it will be very difficult to both keep the door away from the rot-inducing soil, and to make the greenhouse draughtproof.

The receiving wall

The wall to which the greenhouse is attached should, ideally, be absolutely vertical. Unfortunately few walls are. If the wall is less than 12mm out of plumb, the gap can be filled with a bricklaying mortar. But, if it is over 12mm or you do not want a wedge-shaped mortar gap, then you will have to shape three lengths of 50mm × 50mm timber (two vertical battens support the two end frames, and the horizontal batten—the wall plate—supports the roof) so that they form a vertical surface to which the greenhouse frame will be attached. Use a scribing technique to transfer the wall profile on to the timber: hold the wood vertically against the wall and scribe down its length using a pencil attached to a block of wood, which you run down the wall. Saw or plane down the scribed line. Lay a thick layer of sealing mastic or compound along the wall and the timber where the surfaces will meet, screw the timber firmly to the wall with wall plugs or large bolts.

Construction

All the joints should be both glued and screwed, using a PVA waterproof adhesive and either brass, galvanized or japanned screws. The glass or PVC sheeting can be housed either between narrow wooden battens or in glazing grooves cut with a plough plane, router or power saw (fig. 9).

Assembly

Drill the back plate of one end frame and fix it to the vertical timber attached to the wall, then do the same at the other end frame. Move the front frame into place, drilling

and fixing the base to the bolts (which are set in concrete). Drill and screw the ends of the front frame to the respective front timbers of the end frames. The shell of the greenhouse is then ready to receive the roof frame. This should be drilled and fixed to the end and front frames as well as to the wall plate and, when fitting it, you should make quite sure that the frame is flush with the wall to avoid distortion.

Cladding with PVC

To clad the frame first lay one sheet of PVC roofing on the ventilator (if fitted), bedding it down on foam eaves filler and fixing it with screws and washers. Then fix the casement stay and hinges. Carefully position and secure the remainder of the PVC sheets to the roof, using eaves filler, and securing them with screws and washers.

Fix PVC sheeting to the door frame in the same way as to the ventilator, then fix the door in place, making sure that it opens and closes freely. When covering the ends, it is necessary to measure carefully then cut the PVC sheet to the required shape using a fine-toothed saw.

Glazing

The method of overlapping glass panes is quite simple. First press a bed of putty along the glazing beading shelf, then press the bottom pane of glass into the putty. Press from the edges of the pane, not the centre, or it may shatter. Now hold the next higher pane where it will be fixed, and mark the sides of the structure where the bottom of the pane will be located.

Put the pane aside for the time being and drive a 25mm nail into each side of the woodwork immediately next to the lower pane, level with the marks, until just about 6mm of the head is still protruding. You now have two metal stops on which the next pane can rest while it is puttied in position. The process is repeated for successive panes. There are several types of proprietary clips that are made for joining overlapping glass sheets, but they all suffer from the same disadvantage—the final pane often has to be cut to fit. The nail method, on the other hand, allows you as little or as much overlap as you need.

Where a structure abuts against a wall you must provide a run-off for rainwater at the junction point. This flashing could be zinc, lead or copper fitted in a groove cut in a mortar joint, but a simpler alternative is to use self-adhesive flashing, which you simply press into the angle over a coat of flashing primer.

Door catches, handles and the ventilator stay add the finishing touches, along with weatherboarding, which should be nailed over the roof ends and then treated with preservative.

Variations on the theme

Mini greenhouse: A smaller version of the lean-to greenhouse, this is tended from the outside and has one or more opening doors at the front. Usually, this type of greenhouse is essentially a modified lean-to in which similar methods of construction to the basic design are used, with twin doors placed centrally and no end door.

The internal height should be at least 1500mm so that shelving can be fitted to double the effective area, allowing 700mm headroom for the plants situated on each level.

Apex or span: This is a free-standing model which rises to a central ridge and it can be constructed along the lines of two lean-to's placed back to back.

The necessary modifications include a central ridge with capping, a central door in one end, and side and end bracing to provide rigidity.

An alternative design

The glazed and boarded greenhouse illustrated (right) has been designed very simply so that it can be constructed with a minimum of time and effort. The generous eaves height of 1520mm and a ridge height of 2130mm ensures adequate headroom, especially around the edges at bench or staging level where plants are sited. And the width of 2330mm allows considerable freedom of movement.

The timber section for the standard-sized greenhouse should be at least 50mm × 50mm for all structural components and 75mm × 50mm for the door posts. The door battens should be 25mm × 25mm and the glazing beading should be 16mm × 16mm.

The measurements can be adapted according to your requirements, especially the length. If the design is extended in this way some extra reinforcing will be necessary mid-way along the roof and side. A glazing bar can be replaced by a 75mm × 50mm timber and a cross bar at the side would add rigidity and strength. A similar stout piece of timber should be inserted mid-way along the side section.

Throughout the design two main glass widths—460mm and 610mm—are used. The window and roof glass, it must be noted, is installed in 'modules' as nearly square as possible. This means in effect that the glass is panelled. For instance, on the roof each run of glass between timbers consists of four panes of overlapping glass.

In the case of a PVC-sheet-clad greenhouse (below) the timber section should be at least 50mm × 50mm. The hardwood corner posts should be 75mm × 75mm, but you can get away with 50mm × 25mm for the wall plate and vertical wall timbers.

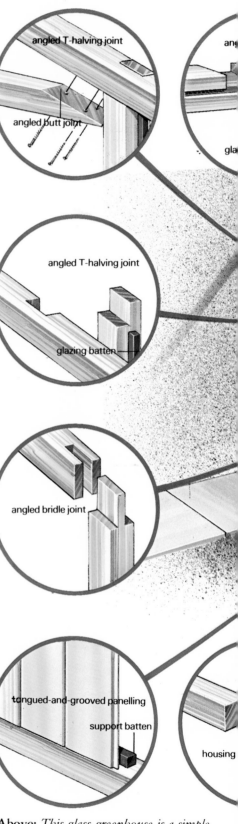

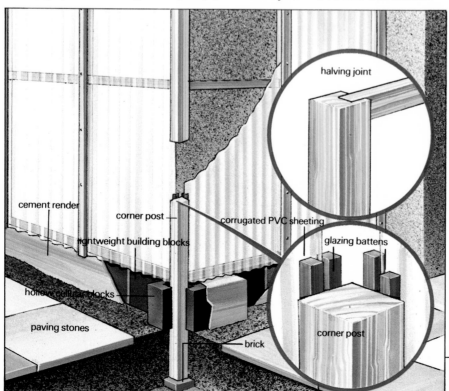

Above: *This glass greenhouse is a simple construction and can be built quickly. A PVC sheet clad greenhouse (left) features slightly different timber sections*

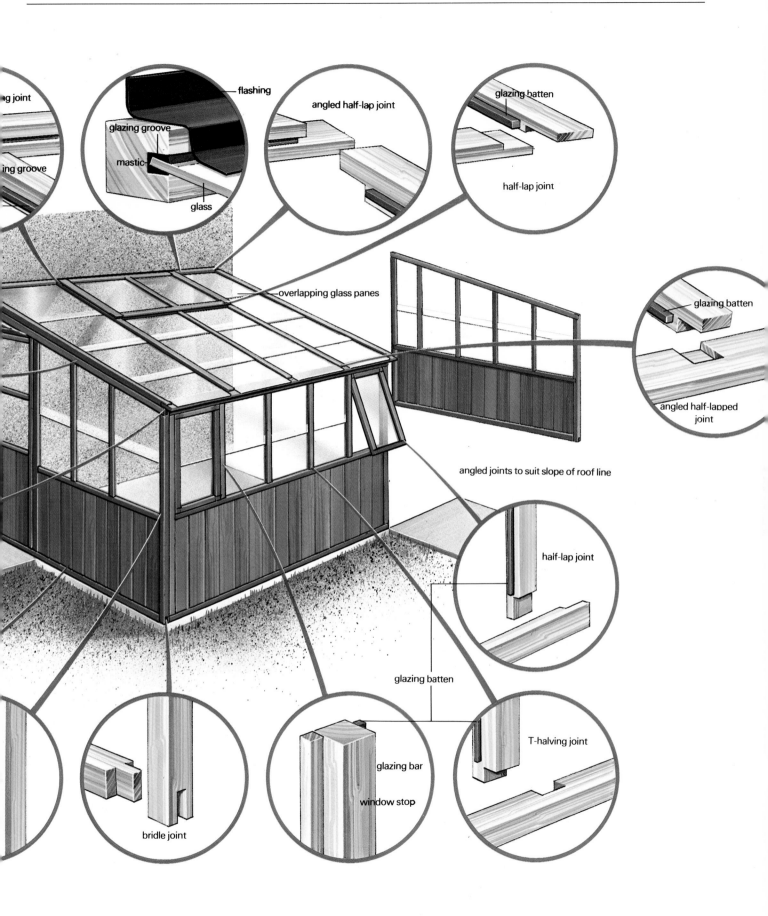

flashing

glazing groove

mastic

glass

angled half-lap joint

glazing batten

half-lap joint

overlapping glass panes

glazing batten

angled half-lapped joint

angled joints to suit slope of roof line

half-lap joint

glazing batten

glazing bar

window stop

bridle joint

T-halving joint

ig joint

ing groove

INDEX